Between You and You

Dr. J. J. McMahon

PAULIST PRESS
New York/Ramsey/Toronto

Library of Congress
Catalog Card Number: 79-89628

ISBN: 0-8091-0300-1

Published by Paulist Press
Editorial Office: 1865 Broadway, New York, N.Y.. 10023
Business Office: 545 Island Road, Ramsey, N.J. 07446

Printed and bound in the
United States of America

Part One

OPENING YOUR EYES

1. I Just Don't Know What to Do

Jean was an attractive young woman completing her master's degree. She had no desire to live. When she was a freshman in college she tried to take her life. She never completely pulled out of her emotional tailspin. Although she derived some satisfaction from her intellectual life, depression permeated most of her days. When she was in her last year of high school she suffered severe emotional damage from having an abortion. From that time her relationships with men always compounded her feeling of emptiness. Now in graduate school she was again roaming the plains of desolation. "If life is the feeling of emptiness, why not empty myself of life?" she reasoned. "Death is the logical solution for ending my misery."

The idea of death made sense to Jean. Death would be the ultimate relief from the pressure pushing down on her head and pushing out from her heart. All those sleepless nights would end with one final sleep. All those dashed desires for a happy life would be put to rest for good. All those guilt feelings about not living well would not survive the final act of not living well. Death is so reasonable. Death is so attractive.

Jean's emotional life was a shopping bag filled with cancerous feelings. She did not experience any excitement in cultural or social activities. Even the beauty of nature appeared bland to her. She was only aware of the changes taking place in her rapidly deteriorating

3

personality. Because she was focusing all her attention on her feelings of loneliness and emptiness, she was destroying her power of perception. This phenomenon is similar to looking directly at the sun. Afterward your vision of the world around you is distorted. Jean's power to perceive herself accurately was almost completely debilitated.

She could not or would not recall those memories of herself when she was enthusiastic about the wonders of nature. Frequently she used to escape city life to enjoy the burgeoning spring foliage or the panoramic view of the brilliant red, golden, and orange autumn leaves. Her concern for others was snuffed out by the tears of her self-pity. She no longer recalled those feelings of fulfillment when she achieved academically. Nor did she take comfort in knowing that she was intelligent. She felt that there was no use in reviving those positive memories, because they would only build up false hopes.

Jean's confusion and depression did not just happen. She was carrying on an internal dialogue whose conclusions accounted for her dire emotional consequences. Her girlfriend persisted in her efforts to help Jean develop a positive view of life. Jean accepted her invitation to attend a weekend open-discussion group. She thoroughly enjoyed the experience of sharing and listening to other people's frustrations and insights about life. Upon some reflection she decided to continue her search for meaning with the leader of the group on a weekly basis. After ten sessions Jean's attitude toward herself and men became optimistic. During those ten weeks she discovered that all her past self-talk was based on many erroneous assumptions about life. Once her silent and distorted ideas of happiness and love were challenged, she saw that they were senseless. In dialoguing with herself she developed a new vision about her life. Within three years she was happily married with two children. A woman at the brink of death turned her mind around and brought life into the world.

The following assumptions were at the root of Jean's negative feelings:
1. "To feel good about myself I *must* be loved by a certain person."

2. "To be interested I must have excitement."
3. "My whole life was wrapped up in _____. When I lost _____ I lost everything."
4. "There is nothing out there for me."
5. "To feel good about myself, I *must* be successful."
6. "To feel good about myself, I have to do everything perfectly."

Let's take a close look at these statements.

1. "To feel good about myself I *must* be loved by a certain person."

Knowing that someone values you reinforces your own feelings of self-worth, but that knowledge does not *cause* you to feel good about yourself. You confuse the ideas of cause and reinforcement when you accept the assumption that your worth depends on someone's love for you. Examine some examples closely and discover the contradictions. Have you loved people who do not feel good about themselves? If love causes another person to feel valuable, why hasn't your love changed them?

Were there times when you were depressed, yet you knew that someone loved you? Even if you had been rejected by certain people close to you, yet you knew that other people accepted you. The plain fact is that other people care for you and yet you are depressed. People are always being loved in some degree. There is hardly anybody completely isolated from everyone's thought, respect, and care. But if everyone is loved minimally there should be no depression.

You feel depressed because you choose not to love yourself—that is, to know yourself and to accept the responsibility of choosing your actions. You prefer to avoid the work required to build a vivacious personality. Instead, you opt to feel sorry about yourself.

You are caught in one of those vicious circles.

Nobody loves me. Why?

Because I guess I'm no good. Why?

Because nobody loves me.

The assumption that "I must be loved" is false, not because you do not want to be loved, nor because no one loves you. The assumption is false because "I *must* be loved" is an absolute command. *Must* means no choice. But love means to choose to give. If you demand that someone loves you, you rob them of their free choice to respond spontaneously to you. If you take away the possibility of love, and at the same time you make your self-worth depend on someone loving you, you are caught in an absurd situation ending in frustration and depression. The more you demand love the more love seems to be pulled away from you.

You may try to convince yourself intellectually that someone else's love makes people what they are. There are many chichés to support your claim of the erroneous assumption—"I *must* be loved to feel good about myself." The true meaning of that assumption is an emotional statement crying out—"I must be noticed to prove to myself that I am worth something." You doubt your own worth because you have not taken the time to learn about yourself. Each time that you felt confused or challenged, you chose the easy way out of your problem by allowing yourself to be dependent on someone else's money, someone else's power, someone else's mind, or someone else's body. When you let other people do your thinking, you will inevitably feel unsure of yourself.

2. "To be interested I *must* have excitement."

This erroneous assumption implicitly states that you are basically passive. Because you have the habit of confusing the idea of interest with the idea of entertainment, your life will be dull most of the time.

Most people want to be interested in something, but they don't know how. While giving a workshop to young adults, I asked the participants to list in order their major concerns. "Not interested enough" or "not interested at all in anything" was on almost everyone's list. Although each one wanted *to get* interested in something, they all said that most things bored them. The silent assumption behind their statements was, "Something exciting causes me to be interested." Now the question was, what qualifies as exciting? Something out of the ordinary? Like what? The moon landing, a cruise around the world, a handsome man, a glamorous woman, skiing in Switzerland, an exciting career, an interesting person.

Behind every great man there is a loving wife.

A child's life is determined by his or her parents' love.

These are the illogical arguments distracting you from the hidden meaning.

All of these people, things, and events may attract your attention but they do not cause your interest. If you were not already interested in sports and adventure, skiing in Switzerland would mean nothing to you. If you were not already interested in sex and love, a handsome man or a glamorous woman would not be exciting. If you were not interested in creating, a career would not be valuable.

Interest means to choose to invest yourself in those activities which are of value to you. You begin to get interested when you ask yourself what is important to you. The answer to that question depends on the breadth and depth of the vision which you have of yourself. No one can tell you what is important to you. Once you clearly see that you <u>choose your own happiness,</u> you will be motivated to make the practical and difficult decisions to give your time and energy to those activities which will develop your powers of mind, will, and body.

Interest also means to stand between. The world stands between your actual self and your potential self. You are made up of your irrational, rational, and supra-rational tendencies. Your actual self is determined by the tendencies you choose to follow. The world is your perception of external reality. Your potential self is who you can become, as shown in the following diagram:

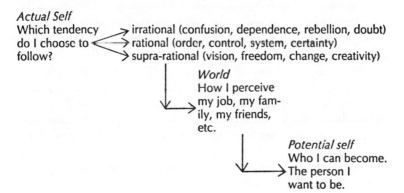

Actual Self
Which tendency → irrational (confusion, dependence, rebellion, doubt)
do I choose to ←→ rational (order, control, system, certainty)
follow? → supra-rational (vision, freedom, change, creativity)

World
How I perceive
my job, my fam-
ily, my friends,
etc.

Potential self
Who I can become.
The person I
want to be.

The answer to the question how to get interested is easy. Pay attention to your best tendencies—to know more, to be free, to create, to do, to be curious, and to give. Behaving according to these tendencies is difficult, because you have to conquer the obstacles of fear and laziness. When you are overly concerned about what others will think of you, your chances of becoming interested in anything are slim. This fear will make you feel shy and uninteresting to the point where you will avoid most social activities.

Frequently, you will settle for boredom by convincing yourself that the things you wanted to do were unrealistic in the first place. A client of mine wanted to become a lawyer. He had some difficulty completing his bachelor's degree because he did not apply himself. However, he was bright. He complained of being bored. When I asked him what steps he had taken to apply for law school, he replied, "None." He told me that he had given up the idea of becoming a lawyer, because it was an unrealistic goal. I told him to look at his goal and his behaviors side by side. Was he saying that his goal was unrealistic because he chose to behave in ways which gave him comfort? Or was he saying that his goal was unrealistic because he was not intellectually capable of achieving it? His goal was realistic. His behavior was unrealistic. Because he developed a pattern of labeling all difficult goals as unrealistic, he was bored. He chose to follow his irrational tendency of being dependent on comfort. The decision to choose and create his future was always open to him. He recognized that fact. He also knew that he was rationalizing his penchant for comfort by labeling arduous goals as unrealistic. His boredom ended when he took himself up on his own challenge to go after what he honestly knew he wanted. Today he is a lawyer.

Both your perception of the world and the idea of who you can be change positively when you decide to act according to your best intuitions. You intuitively know that you can learn more than what you know, feel better than you are feeling, do more than what you are doing, make better decisions than you are making and think better than you are thinking. You also know that, if you will to get what you want, you will get it. When you act on this knowledge you become interesting and exciting.

3. "My whole life is wrapped up in _____. When I lost _____ I lost everything."

Judy was living a pleasant life. She had the job that she wanted in·the place where she wanted it. She also had a rewarding love relationship with John, a company executive. As long as she could please a man in a relationship she felt emotionally satisfied. Eventually, she believed that her happiness depended totally on feeling wanted and approved by the man she loved. Doomsday came for her when John told her that he wanted out. Judy became despondent and listless. Her job was no longer appealing. She believed that her life was wrecked beyond repair because her whole life was wrapped up in John. When she lost John, she thought that she had lost everything.

Another example of this erroneous assumption is the story of Tom who was a New York City fireman. The job was the centerpiece of his life. The educational plans for his children, his wife, and himself depended on the security of his employment. His wife went back to college to prepare herself for a career. Tom was working toward a degree in electrical technology. When they both had achieved their objectives they would be financially able to send their children to college.

They were happy in the pursuit of their goals. Then the unthinkable happened. New York City was on the verge of bankruptcy. Mass layoffs of city employees threw thousands of people into emotional confusion. They asked: How could it happen to me? Why did it happen to me?

Tom found himself on the unemployment line. His wife left school to look for a job. The emotional climate in their home grew tense as Tom vacillated between days of anger and depression. He was becoming unbearable and he knew it. He realized that he had made himself and his whole family totally dependent on his job. When he was laid off, he felt that he had lost everything. This crisis forced him to take a second look at himself. The turning point in his emotional life came when he saw that he had lost *only* something but not everything.

Both the above cases illustrate the negative consequences of assuming that your whole emotional, mental and physical well-being is dependent on someone or some event beyond your control. To allow yourself to think that part of your life is your whole life is to escape your responsibility of knowing and creating yourself. You become identified with the person whom you are pleasing, with the job to which you are devoted, with the company to which you belong, with the university where you teach, with the friends for whom you live, and with the church and country to which you belong. Subtly, your objective in living shifts from doing what is important to you to being accepted by certain people. When you are rejected by that someone else, you feel that there is no purpose to life. But, in fact, before being rejected you had no purpose of your own; however, you did not feel that emptiness because you were comforted by your associations. After being fired, rejected in love, or ostracized by your friends, you feel as though you are dizzily floating in space. You are painfully alone. There is no one and no thing to hold on to. Life is meaningless. Your only relief is to close your eyes.

You can avoid the feelings of depression and loneliness by concentrating your attention on your powers of mind and will. They constitute the center of gravity for your mental and emotional life. Common sense tells you that your whole life can never be surrendered to another person, institution, or ideology. You can never escape the responsibility of knowing and creating yourself. If you erroneously choose to believe that your life is not your own, then you will suffer the negative emotions of that decision, depression and anxiety. If you accept the responsibility to grow in knowledge of yourself, then you will experience the joy of loving yourself and others.

4. "There is nothing out there for me."

Lucy at the age of thirty-eight divorced her husband. Working at a low paying clerical job she was struggling to meet the mortgage payments and feed and clothe her two teenagers. Each day she had that horrible feeling of the weary swimmer going under for the third time. Nevertheless, she managed to secure the necessities of life for herself and her children. Emotionally, she was becoming more depressed. She believed that there was no opportunity for her to rebuild her life. She felt uncomfortable with the idea of meeting new male companions. Her social life dwindled to having lunch with the women at the office. Even though she was intelligent and talented in business ways, she had no hope of advancing herself professionally. The hidden assumption destroying her mental and emotional attitude toward herself was the idea that hope comes when opportunity knocks. The more she thought about her financial and marital difficulties the more she was convincing herself that she was unlucky. She believed that everything was going against her. Her former husband was not contributing to the support of his children. She could not risk moving from her secure but boring and meager paying job in a shaky economy. She was getting older and, so she believed, less attractive. She was thinking herself into states of depression because she was making her feeling of hope dependent on opportunities.

The following is a paraphrasing of our sessions in which she learned how to confront and reject the erroneous assumption contributing to her mental, emotional, and behavioral immobility:

Lucy: There is not much I can do to change my situation.

Counselor: What situation?

Lucy: I don't make enough money. I can't meet anybody.

Counselor: Because . . .

Lucy: Because there is nothing out there for me. I don't have the education to get a better job and look at me. I'm overweight and pushing forty. Who wants me now? I missed all my chances when I was young.

Counselor: Are you saying that you cannot look forward to having joy and happiness in your life?

Lucy: That's right. I missed it all.

Counselor: What is the *it* that you're talking about?

Lucy: All those things that make me happy.

Counselor: What are those things?

Lucy: Well, I guess those things which make me feel secure.

Counselor: Like what?

Lucy: Like money, someone's love and attention.

Counselor: Did you have those things at one time?

Lucy: Yes, I did.

Counselor: Did they make you secure once and for all?

Lucy: I guess not.

Counselor: You feel sad in not having them, but they don't make you secure. If they don't make you secure, what does?

Lucy: I guess I make myself feel secure.

Counselor: When do you feel most secure?

Lucy: When I know I can do the things that I want to do.

Counselor: When you feel confident.

Lucy: That's it. When I believe in myself.

Counselor: In other words, your hope for a happy life depends on believing in yourself.

Lucy: That's right.

Counselor: Then you did not miss *it all* as you said before.

Lucy: I guess not.

Counselor: You guess?

Lucy: No. I'm sure. If I stop thinking that the solutions to my problems depend on everyone except myself, I'll begin to do something.

Counselor: Like what?

Lucy: I can go back to school.
   I can lose weight.
   I can start going out.

Lucy took her own advice. She went back to school, lost fifteen pounds, and found a better paying job.

Hope is essential to change your feelings and behaviors. When you hope, you anticipate the feeling of joy that you will experience after you have achieved your goal. But you cannot anticipate that joy if you have neither vision nor confidence. Unless you use your reason and intuition to know yourself, you will never set any personal or career goals. Without knowledge of yourself, you will not believe in yourself. How can you believe in someone you do not know? And how can you hope for happiness if you do not believe in your own capabilities of knowing and choosing what is best for you?

5. "To feel good about myself I *must* be successful."

You may wonder why wealthy, intelligent, and talented people would commit suicide. From all appearances they possess everything needed to be a success—money, prestige, power, and friends. They achieved what they set out to get. If success makes people feel good about themselves, they should have no reason for ending their lives.

Everyone achieves a measure of success in his life. Reflect for a moment on your own achievements—a high school diploma, a college degree, a graduate degree, an impressive sale, special recognition from your boss, a Christmas bonus, or a merit raise. Ask yourself why you felt so good about yourself at those moments.

Did you feel good about yourself because you deserved to be recognized?

Did you feel good about yourself because you deserved the money?

Did you feel good about yourself because you recalled how adamantly and confidently you pursued your goal?

When you are successful, you feel good about yourself because you recall that you remained faithful to those values which motivated you to achieve your goal. Feeling good about yourself does not depend on the rewards of success. If learning is important to you, you do not forget it after securing a B.A. If loving is important to you, you do not forget it after you are married. If caring for other people is important to you, you do not forget it after making a few friends. If achieving is important to you, you do not forget it after your first promotion.

When you become drunk with the rewards of success, you believe that you need them to feel good about yourself. Your condition becomes similar to that of the alcoholic. He believes he needs alcohol to survive emotionally. The more he drinks, the more he needs a drink. The more he needs a drink, the less he feels good about himself. Likewise, developing a dependency on the rewards of success is courting self-destruction.

Once you make success an absolute requirement for feeling a sense of self-worth, you are nothing until you attain it. But as long as you feel that you are nothing, you have neither the vision to create worthwhile goals nor the courage to make difficult decisions. By accepting the assumption that you must be successful to feel good about yourself, you get caught in a frustrating logic:

I am nothing without success.

But I am not successful.

Therefore, I am nothing.
But from nothing you get nothing.

6. "To feel good about myself I have to do everything perfectly."

The basic idea behind this self-statement is that you are a bundle of behaviors—nothing more and nothing less. The worth of the whole bundle—you—is determined by the quantity and quality of your behaviors. Your goal then is to amass as many perfect behaviors as you can during the course of a day. In the evening you tally your performances which range from excellent to poor. When someone asks you "Did you have a good day?" that question to you means, "Did you have more plus than minus behaviors today?"

In order to know how well you performed you need some sort of measuring stick. When you say, "I had a good day," that reply could mean any of the following:

"I didn't make any mistakes at work."
"I didn't lose my patience with the children."
"I had a record number of sales."
"I won my tennis match."
"I got along with everyone at work."
"I got along very well with my girlfriend/boyfriend."
"I sold my idea to the executive committee of the company."

These statements contain an implicit goal which is the measure for determining the quality of your behaviors. Unless you analyze these statements to discover what goal is motivating you, you will probably experience more pain than pleasure. Let's take the first statement to illustrate this point:

"I didn't make any mistakes at work."
Your goal may be:

To avoid the criticism of your supervisor
To seek the approval of your co-workers
To build up your ego
To feel comfortable and secure in what you are doing
To get a promotion (being successful)

The equation goes something like this:

Feeling good about yourself = having a good day = avoiding mistakes = receiving comfort, approval, or success.

When you say that to feel good about yourself you must do whatever you are doing perfectly, you more accurately mean that you feel good when you receive approval or comfort. Avoiding mistakes is the way to get that comfort or approval. Doing things perfectly in that sense is a negative concept, because it means behaving in a certain way to avoid pain. As a child in school, you learned this distorted way of thinking because you practiced avoiding mistakes to escape shame and criticism. Intellectually you were improving, but your emotional life was deteriorating. After years of practice you perfect the art of avoiding mistakes. The phrase "avoiding mistakes" means avoiding discomfort by doing what is expected of you.

If you accept this line of reasoning, you will suffer anxiety and may eventually develop an ulcer. Whenever you make a mistake— that is, you lose approval, comfort or success—you begin to believe that you cannot do anything right because you have no abilities. In other words, you are saying that you are what you do. Add that assumption to the above equation of feeling good about yourself, and you will have developed the perfect internal self-destruct mental time bomb. As soon as you make your first mistake, you believe that you are no good. You lose confidence. But how can you avoid mistakes in the future when you have no confidence in yourself in the present? Your good days will be the ones which you spend in bed.

Your anxiety can be traced to your faulty assumption that to feel good about yourself you must perform perfectly. If you analyze that assumption you will see that you are following your tendency to be dependent on someone to give you a reward, such as recognition, for doing something well. Recognition is nice to have, but you are not dependent on it to feel good about yourself. Choosing dependency over freedom is the real cause of your anxiety. The more you exercise your freedom of choice to do what is important to you, the less you will experience anxiety. However, to behave freely requires effort and frequently involves discomfort. But the reward of freedom is to feel genuinely good about yourself.

How to get out of confusion

When you are confused you probably say one of two things to yourself:

"I don't know what I'm doing."
"I don't know where I'm going."

To get rid of your anxious feelings try:

1. Retreating: Remove yourself mentally and physically from your immediate surroundings. Go to a place that is pleasant and refreshing. For some, that place might be the seashore; for others, it might be the mountains. Drink in the beauty, peace and power of the environment.
2. Get specific. Ask yourself the following questions:
   How do I want to feel about myself? (Some answers might be: strong, confident, independent, etc.)
   How do I want to feel toward others? (Some answers might be: honest, open.)
   What kind of activities do I enjoy? (Some answers might be: reading, building things, socializing, painting, etc.)
3. Imagine yourself in specific situations in which you are feeling the way you want to feel about yourself, doing what you enjoy doing, and feeling toward certain people the way you want to feel.
4. Identify everyone and everything which distracts you from doing what *you* want to do and from feeling the way *you* want to feel. Ask yourself questions similar to the following:
   Do you allow your parents to confuse you because you rely more on their judgments than on your own judgments?
   Do you allow your spouse, girlfriend, boyfriend, or friends to confuse you because you are trying to live up to what they all expect from you?
   Does your religion confuse you because you do not understand why it obliges you to live according to certain rules?

These exercises will help you to take charge of your thinking. Once you know *what* you want, then you know *where* you are going. The first step in learning *how* to advance to where you want to go is to know the obstacles in your way. Now, you are on your way toward putting order and vision in your life.

The Art of Listening to Yourself

Dialogue 1—Clarifying what confuses you

Confusion is the feeling of simultaneously wanting to go some-where and not being able to move. You do not know which way to go because either you are pulled in different directions, or you are not sure where you are standing. For example, which way do you move when at the same time the doorbell rings, the phone rings, and the toast pops up? Or which way do you go when, having left the train, you do not recognize the subway station?

Emotional, mental and behavioral confusion is a state of dishar-mony. You may want to behave a certain way, but your feelings are pulling you in the opposite direction. Mentally you are mixed up because you speak to yourself inconsistently. One day you tell yourself that such and such a philosophy is a good way to live, and the next day you change your mind. The confused person experi-ences himself as someone stuck in molasses. He wants to pop free from his confusion, but he does not know how to do it.

1. Reflect on each of the following concerns for a moment. Men-tally, check your state of mind about each one.

Concern	Confused	Doubtful	Clear
Money			
Pleasure			
Career			
Marriage			
Love			
Trust			
Sex			
Friendship			
Religion			
Future			
Parenting			
Who am I?			
(Other concerns)			

2. Describe concretely to yourself each experience about which you are confused or doubtful. For example: I don't feel free in my marriage. I feel like I'm doing a job. I do what I am supposed to do, but I'm bored.

3. Imagine yourself going through those experiences of confusion now. Pay close attention to what you are *feeling* and *saying to yourself*. For example: Love—Here I am giving myself unselfishly to my girlfriend by doing what she wants me to do, and she takes me for granted. I feel like nothing. She should show me more attention.

4. Which of the following feelings do you experience most when you are confused?

   Anxiety
   Anger
   Depression
   Fear
   Being left out
   Frustration
   Hostility
   Jealousy
   Shyness
   Inferiority

5. Clarify those experiences filling you with confusion by labeling your concerns, feelings and self-statements. For example: I am confused about my relationship with my boyfriend. I feel lonely and I tell myself that he should show me more attention. I don't know if continuing the relationship is right or wrong for me.

6. Now check those silent assumptions underlying your concerns. Do any of the assumptions listed on pages 3 and 4 account for your negative feelings?

2. I Have to Get Myself Together

Rules, routines, and rigid daily timetables are the contents of the metaphysical glue barely holding together the emotional lives of some people. Getting their lives together means putting their behaviors in order. They rarely change the sequence of their daily activities, and practically never change their ideas about the rightness of their routine. Adamantly, they justify their ideology because their emotional life hangs in the balance. Imposing a new system of behavior on yourself definitely helps you to escape the constant emotional dizziness that you experience when you have lost your direction; however, unless your order is monitored by critical thinking you will slip back into foggy confusion.

The following anecdote illustrates the poor judgment of those who worship the idol of thoughtless order. Each semester college students suffer the ordeal of registration. Registering ten thousand people within a week is a logistical feat. Order, system, discipline, and communication are essential in controlling large numbers of people. The dean in charge of administration at a large university planned registration with the enthusiasm of a general about to launch a crucial campaign. Every detail was double-checked so that the long lines of students would move smoothly through his maze of bureaucratic checkpoints. One day I, as a young administrator, was supervising the movement of students at the cashier booths located in the auxiliary gym overflowing with a thousand people who were cranky from the noise, crowding, and heat. Suddenly, a middle-aged woman on one of the lines collapsed. I rushed to her. Crouched over her was her husband. He told me that his wife had a history of heart trouble. This unfortunate incident stopped the flow of traffic momentarily. About ten yards away the dean of administration, appearing annoyed at the woman on the floor, shouted to the people on line to keep moving. The woman's husband and I carried her off to the side of the gym where she awaited an ambulance. The dean complimented me on my rescue operation which would be written up in a letter of commendation for my personnel file. I thought he was pleased because I might have helped save the woman's life, but he was actually feeling relieved because in his mind I saved the registration lines from being thrown into disarray.

At times you may experience the compulsion for order taking over your life. Just as the dean in the story was so fixed on order that he could not see people, so also you might be insensitive to anyone who disrupts your routine. Feeling good about yourself may depend on accomplishing the things that you are supposed to do. If your actions are guided by law, you feel satisfied when you comply with certain rules of behavior. Knowing that you have done the right thing puts your mind at rest. To illustrate the satisfaction enjoyed by the ordered person, let's take the conflict arising between authority and your individual rights. Theoretically, it is easy to see that legitimate authority does not always act for the individual's good. However, in practice you accept this assumption uncritically because in obeying authority you are rewarded with tranquillity. For example, at work you suppress your freedom and intelligence to reap the rewards dispensed by a gracious boss. Your life on the job is pleasant when you avoid conflict. So, you will mind your business. You will speak, but your words are chatter. When you go home you will have your chance to be boss. Then, the members of the family will sacrifice their intelligence and freedom for the sake of peace.

Besides obeying external regulations you learn to follow your own internal authority, which gives you a sense of contentment. For example, you tell yourself that you must be loyal to your friends. You must not be angry. You must be faithful to your spouse. You must be perfect. If you measure up to the laws you make for yourself, you feel satisfied. However, if you break these laws you feel guilty. You feel guilty because you have done something wrong, that is, you transgressed your own commands. If you have an extramarital relationship, you feel guilty because you broke the rule commanding you not to have sexual intercourse outside of marriage.

However, many of your guilt feelings can be traced to shallow thinking. Authentic satisfaction and tranquillity are not the result of obeying laws, and guilt is not the result of breaking laws. Often you feel a false guilt because you have reduced your reality. By that I mean that you have taken the freedom and novelty out of your life and have made life a series of routine things to do. You can expect nothing new. There is no depth or excitement in yourself and others. Feelings based on a shrunken reality are not healthy. You may feel satisfied with yourself because you have never been unfaithful, but you may have missed the wider reality of love. You may feel satisfied with yourself because you were always loyal to your bosses, but you may have lost the deeper reality of self-knowledge. I am not suggesting that you be unfaithful or ornery, but I am saying that you are not guaranteed a genuine feeling of being alive by the strict observance of rules and regulations.

When the laws of the ordered person are subservient to one's critical thinking, a code of behaviors can nurture authentic feelings. Laws are dependent on the vision you have of reality. As you develop your insights about yourself and others, you modify your self-commands. True guilt, then, is the feeling of emptiness and darkness resulting from your mental laziness.

Steps in developing true order

1. Spotting the real problem

Be problem-oriented in your thinking. Push aside the negative feelings caused by mental confusion so that you may immediately focus on the contradictions which you experience. Be aware of the difference between your thoughts and your behaviors. Recognize that your rigid thinking accounts for most of your negative feelings. You will discover that the real contradiction causing your confusion exists within yourself.

2. Getting at the important matters

In more complex matters analytical skills are required to bring about order. Often, value conflicts throw you into states of mental and emotional confusion. As much as you want to act in a given situation you are immobilized by your indecisiveness. You cannot decide what to do because two or more fundamental principles lead to seemingly contradictory conclusions. When a country demands a certain behavior from its citizens, you at times find yourself in the predicament of being faithful to your country but untrue to yourself or vice versa. Or the situation may be one in which you are torn between family loyalty and the achievement of your personal goals. In either case begin to categorize what is personally, socially, and/or religiously important to you. Then put your values in an order of priority.

3. Building a priority of values

Establishing an order of values presupposes more than sorting out and labeling your ideas and behaviors. Constructing a true system of values requires intuitive thought. Unless you are able to see what is truly important to you, your values will be conventional or arbitrary. By looking more closely at your ideas and behaviors you have prepared the ground for order and control. But the quality of your order depends on the purpose of that order. Without a vision of rock bottom values, the order you establish will be superficial. *Know what you believe*

4. The mark of a good judgment

A true judgment which solves your problem is one which produces mental and emotional harmony. For example, the resolution of the conflict between personal conscience and loyalty is motivated by your desire for internal unity. You want to feel, think, and behave congruently. Only a vital and internal principle of order can help you achieve your goal. All your ideas, behaviors, and feelings will fit together in an organic whole according to a system of values based on your vision of what is honestly important to you. Importance tells you why to plunge yourself into life each day with a hundred percent effort. Your judgments organize your thoughts, feelings, and behaviors around the centerpiece of what is important to you. That is why the answer to what is important to you is so consequential for your happiness.

5. An ongoing process

Because you understand and live your existence in the light of what is most important to you, you are on your guard against a "once and for all" type of thinking. If you freeze your system of values or philosophy at any point in your life, you cut yourself off from the mental activity which is so necessary to enrich your days.

A static philosophy of life dams up your deep feelings for life. You are left with your flat and empty concepts. Your ideas become the molds which shape your behaviors and feelings. You are convinced that you can solve the major problems in your life with a few good ideas. These ideas work for some people because they have reduced life to the microscopic dimensions of their cheap concepts. The word "work" is deceiving. In this case it means that your ideas get results because you have eliminated the difficult questions about life. You have whittled down the number and the importance of major questions about life to accommodate your ready-made answers. But in reality you are continually attached to all life. That is why the answer to what is important is never final for you. The spontaneity and novelty of life always teaches you something more about yourself.

6. Thinking shapes your feelings

Practicing rational thought processes is essential for establishing emotional order in your life. Using the pragmatic method of clearly stating your problem, attentively sorting out your ideas and behaviors, forming new ideas, and testing your ideas produces a sound philosophy for guiding your life. You become a more understanding and creative person to the degree that you faithfully carry on an internal dialogue about important questions. Your insights will give you a renewed appreciation of each question you asked.

Checking the order in your life

Is the order of your life a timetable? For example: I get up at 6:30, I shower, I dress, I walk the dog, I eat, I go to work, I eat lunch at 12:00, I work, I eat dinner at 6:30, I watch TV, I go to bed.

Do you feel very upset if your timetable is interrupted—for example, if your alarm clock does not go off when it should?

Do you believe that your daily schedule must be the way it is because that's the way life is?

When the day is over do you feel satisfied because everything went right, that is, you did everything you were supposed to do according to your schedule?

If your answer is yes to each of these questions, then your order is blinding you. Your timetable is like a big maze through which you pass daily. With practice you can go through a whole day with a blindfolded mind. The only purpose of your order is to protect you from the inconvenience of thinking.

Now ask yourself the following questions.

Do you have a clear purpose for the order in your life? For example, I have arranged my home life in a certain way so that the members of the family can grow in love and knowledge of each other.

I have arranged my career life in a way so that I may be more productive.

Have you changed the order in your life when you thought it was not helping you to enjoy what was important to you?

If you answered yes to these questions then you have a positive idea about order. Your power of vision is governing your idea of order.

The Art of Listening to Yourself

Dialogue 2—Checking the motives of your actions

If you observe your behaviors from day to day, you will see that there is a pattern to your life. As far as your behaviors are concerned one day is very much like the next. Even when your routine is interrupted by holidays and vacations, you do pretty much the same things you did on previous days off. The order of your life is determined by fundamental decisions which you have made. For example, in choosing marriage and/or a particular career you elected a pattern of behaviors for your love life and/or your work life. Your fundamental decisions concerning your relationships, religion, intellectual life, and leisure time shape your behaviors. Ordinarily your life follows a plan. However, if you are confused about an important matter, then you feel out of order.

1. Reflect for a moment on each major activity of your life. Which behaviors do you avoid and which do you enjoy?

   Work
   Planning your work
   Improving your abilities through education
   Trying something new
   Looking for advancement
   Establishing friendships with other workers

   Marriage
   Sharing your ideas
   Doing things together
   Sex
   Listening to spouse
   Planning the future

   Relationships
   Giving my time
   Listening
   Taking the initiative to plan activities
   Making new friends

   Religion
   Thinking about it
   Practicing it

   Other

2. Discover your motives for avoiding positive behaviors in each activity by spotlighting the statements you make to yourself. For example: I avoid *trying something new at work* because *I feel afraid of making a mistake.*

3. Find the hidden irrational assumption underlying your reason for avoiding positive behaviours. For example: *I feel afraid of making a mistake* assumes that:

A. Mistakes in life are not allowed.

B. My reputation will be completely destroyed with one mistake.

C. I *must* do everything perfectly.

3. The Light Begins to Dawn

Timon, an attractive twenty-five-year-old woman, seeking the fullness of life, wrapped up her belongings, bid farewell to Belgium, and headed for Paris in the autumn of 1967. Prepared as a school teacher, she encountered more than her share of obstacles in finding a position in the business world. After a couple of months of fruitless interviews and cheap cafeteria food, she finally landed a job as a copyeditor for a publishing company. Now that the appetizer had arrived the delicious entrée of excitement would follow soon. Her social life picked up momentum. Within a few months her hunger for happiness drove her into a frenzied search for *l'amour*. Romantic interludes with one man were no longer satisfying. She plunged herself into almost daily amorous affairs. The full life began to taste bitter.

In the spring of 1968, depressed, Timon escaped Paris in her MG sportscar. While motoring through the countryside on her way to Belgium, she mused about her fantasies of the good life. Her thoughts were interrupted by the honking horn of a passing car. The honking continued. Timon glanced to her left to see what was the matter. The passerby flashed a smile and a seductive wink. Her acknowledging wink encouraged him to continue his odd, difficult, but seemingly rewarding sign language. Within a few moments Timon was following the curious stranger down a side road leading them to an inn where they talked about the meaning of life, dined, and bedded down for the evening. On the following day Timon was on her way back to Paris where she would rejoin her highway lover as soon as he finished his business in a nearby town. For the next two weeks her days were filled with the joys of romance. The simple pleasures of walking along the banks of the Seine, frolicking in the park, and sharing a carafe of wine at a sidewalk cafe tingled Timon's romantic sentiments. However, little by little, suspicions, doubts, and boredom seeped into their relationship. The cracks foreshadowing the impending destruction were evident.

One evening as Timon was pensively sipping her coffee at the cafe, Mark, a friend from her first days in Paris, spotted her. In the autumn of 1967 they were both strangers in the city of love, he pursuing an advanced degree in psychology at the university and she pursuing life. From time to time they saw one another, but always as friends. This chance meeting buoyed Timon's spirit. They talked about love. Mark, sensing her confusion, suggested to Timon that perhaps she had been cutting the flowers from the tree of love without caring for its life. Just as the roots of a tree reach deep and wide to nourish and strengthen it in all seasons, so also human beings nurture the relationship of love by deepening their respect, understanding, and knowledge of each other in the soil of honest dialogue. Timon was struck by this image. She clearly saw that her idea of the full life was nothing more than a series of shallow and evanescent relationships leaving her confused and empty. Realizing that achieving happiness is more than simply plucking it, Timon resolved to develop a more mature view of life which included accepting her responsibility for choosing values.

Timon's open conversation with Mark fanned the dying embers of her philosophical vision. She knew that the tree of the full life could grow only in the fertile ground of her own spirit. Having plowed and harrowed the fields of her mind, she sowed the seeds of love and responsibility. Within a year she reaped the harvest of a rewarding relationship which has been fruitful for a decade.

The meaning of vision

Your day-to-day responsibilities meld into one another so routinely that after a while one day is just like the next. The people and the events in your life become a parade of shadows. How often do you reduce all people to a common denominator? A "you've seen one, you've seen them all" mentality sizes up your fellow man. How often do you tell yourself that the more the world changes the more it is the same? And how often do you feel that your existence is a matter of marking time? The melancholy of boredom is the disease of the intellectually blind: Only vision can restore vitality to your existence.

When you chance to meet people of vision, their enthusiasm startles your sluggish mind. You intuitively know that these people are alive. They are not shadows. Their zest for living jolts you out of your dull existence. There are many contemporaries who are living rejections to the theory that life is business as usual. Unless you are totally encrusted by routine, you recognize that these people see what life is. Your recognition of their vision is an explicit admission on your part that you have the power to see that your existence is more than routine.

The meaning of philosophical vision is not immediately known to you, but its existence is directly felt within you. If you examine some outstanding people in the history of ideas, you will learn what this vision means. For example, Plato was a brilliant literary man of his day. His memory continues in history because he reached for the answers that would give meaning to his daily living. His works speak about the lasting ideas which are applicable in every age. Plato's vision of truth helps man understand the nature of order. For him absolute goodness is the purpose for all order.

Just as Plato engaged in a dialogue with himself to answer important existential questions, such as the meaning of justice, truth, and knowledge, so you also must rationally address yourself to important questions. Analyzing the enduring questions leads you to conclusions about the content of your life. For example, if you think that your existence is more than matter, then you know that human destiny extends beyond this material world. If you do not believe in life after death, then the meaning of your life must be discovered in the daily experience of yourself. In either case the order which you design for your everyday life will be based on what you are living for. Vision is the power to see which realities give meaning to your life. It may be freedom, love, justice, money, or power. The activity of pushing your mind to decide what is truly important to you is more crucial than determining which goal is more rewarding. Unless you strenuously think through the question of what is most valuable to you, you will not feel any driving force vitalizing your daily activities. But once you see what you are living for, then you unleash within yourself an enormous show of personal strength to make your goal a reality. For example, if you believe that to live means to be free in your feelings, thoughts, and behaviors, then you will strive every day in every way to be yourself.

People of vision constantly seek a deeper and broader understanding of human existence, whereas people without vision reduce the meaning of all reality to their own private interpretation. People without vision are closed-minded. They do not want their worlds disturbed with new ideas. People of vision, however, see themselves as participants in the continuing movement of truth over ignorance. People without vision see themselves as shrewd operators in a competitive world. They often spend valuable time squabbling over minor matters to defend their inflated egos. People of vision on the other hand soar over trivialities. People without vision feed their misguided curiosity on the confused and neurotic behaviors of their neighbors. This is one reason why soap operas are so popular. Viewers want the confusion to thicken. They could spend years watching a family committing mental and emotional suicide. Why? Because they identify their own self-defeating attitudes with those of the performers.

People of vision clearly see the weighty matters in a situation. Knowing what is important in a human problem is half the solution. However, you can only decide what is important in a particular situation after you have developed a comprehensive view of life. The power of vision helps you to develop this view.

The practical value of vision

Erroneously, many people think that the philosophically minded are impractical. People of vision are dismissed as wide-eyed idealists. An example of an interpersonal problem will show how a philosophy of life effectively solves a conflict. Experiencing the demise of your marriage or a close relationship is a painful event. Often the partners gnaw at each other's person over petty matters. Conversations drift into arguments. Discussions become debates. The relationship degenerates into patterns of self-defense. Harmless words are interpreted negatively. Innocent behaviors are viewed suspiciously. "Why am I reacting this way?" you begin to ask yourself. "What happened over the years?" The answer is: Nothing happened. You failed to grow intellectually and emotionally. You have become discontented and self-centered in your search for comfort. Your partner's words and behaviors have become annoying. In fact, most events and people may annoy you. Your petulant behavior results from your narrow idea of the way you think the world should be. Because your partner does not measure up to your subjective standards, you judge him or her not to be worthy of your respect.

In contrast, people who have developed a philosophical perspective on life view interpersonal conflicts as opportunities for growing in knowledge of oneself and the other. They want to arrive at the heart of the problem, whereas the unthinking partners in a marriage are often caught up in negative talk centering on jealousy, one's own comfort, or the other's oppressive ways. The thinking partners are focusing on the achievement of mutual goals or individual personal goals. Their discussions center on clarifying the ways by which they will intellectually and emotionally grow together. Neither wants to control the other. They both want to move to a more enriched level of existence. Positive thinking strengthens the love of a relationship, because each person draws on each other's power of vision.

Seeing what is important to you develops strength of will. Characteristically, people committed to their understanding of reality are forceful in word and demeanor. They speak with an internal authority. They themselves are the living proof of what they say. Confused and uncommitted people fade into the nondescript world of shadows. But people of vision make a mark on the world by their presence. How often have you said that you were impressed by such and such a person even though you may have forgotten his words? You did not forget him because his words conveyed the power of his freedom and vision. You recognized in him the qualities of character that you yourself want.

Their trust in life is the feeling of resiliency. No mattter what adversities confront people of vision, they come through their troubles with greater power. They are ready to meet new challenges. Their means of power and success is their trust in their drive to live. They know that their lives are rooted in all life. If you reflect for a moment you will see that you are not isolated from the current of vital power coursing through the world. You are connected to the power of the artist, the engineer, the politician, the writer, and everyone else through your knowledge about them. You can learn to do what they have done. Also, all of nature is a graphic reminder that we all share in growth, power, and beauty. People of vision draw their strength from the belief that the power to grow humanly resides in them. They have only to make up their minds to use it. Consequently they are confident that they will prevail over any difficulty.

The vision that your life is connected to the source of life has practical consequences. At times you are tempted to give up the good fight in your quest for a happy life. On the job you may suffer injustices. At home you may be treated indifferently. In the world you witness man's inhumanity to man. You conclude that there is no hope for a happy life or a better world. So you think that the best you can do is shield yourself from pain. Finally, your emotional life becomes bland.

In contrast, the trusting person perceives these injustices within a broad perspective. He is not willing to be anyone's victim. For example, the employee realizes that the meaning of his life is not completely dependent on his superior's approval. The demise of this relationship is not the end of his world. If the boss is persistently unreasonable, instead of being timid and whining, the employee, trusting his tendency to be his own person, becomes assertive and rational in rectifying the injustice. In the event the employer responds negatively, what will the employee lose? He might lose a raise, a promotion, or even a job. But if the employee accepts the injustice, what might he himself lose? Perhaps he may forfeit his self-respect, his trust in life, and maybe eventually his job through his own lack of enthusiasm.

Fearful and complaining people drag themselves through each day without any hope that their home, career, and social situation will improve. But people who know what is important to them as human beings reap the rewards of confidence and courage. The immediate reward of responding to what is important to you is the feeling of hope. Hope is knowing that your future is the unfolding of your present. Each decision that you make today will have negative or positive consequences for the future. Therefore, your future, just as your present, is your own responsibility. It is senseless to say: "I hope that the future brings me some happiness." In this statement you speak as if everything and everyone except you is responsible for the way that you will feel tomorrow. In fact, there is no future in the sense that there is something out there waiting for you. The future is using your power now to achieve the goals that you want. Tomorrow will be better because you are making better todays.

In addition to the feelings of trust, hope, and courage, vision also produces greatness and calmness of spirit. People of vision have the capacity to genuinely welcome a wide range of personality types. Open-minded and big-hearted people respect and enjoy the diversity within humanity. They respond to different people with characteristically good humor. Each encounter with a new person or idea is an experience of the immensity and novelty of man's spirit. The feeling of newness is the reward of vision.

When you are confused, your responses are stilted. You are not sure how your words and behaviors will be received. Holding back your true opinions by hedging your responses drains your energies. When you do not know what is important to you, you speak hesitantly and apologetically and behave obsequiously. Fear of being rejected or of appearing stupid short-circuits your power to think for yourself. In order to break out of your confusion, you have to direct your reason to assault your nonsensical fears. Only spontaneous verbal and behavioral responses will reinforce your freely inquiring mind. Your active mind in turn will reinforce your spontaneous responses.

In summarizing your thoughts about the effects of vision on your feelings you clearly observe that a critical and searching mind accounts for positive feelings, whereas a defensive and complacent mind breeds negative feelings. In order to advance emotionally and mentally, you need to learn the methods of developing vision.

Three ways of developing vision

1. Intuition

The problem of escaping your mental and emotional confusion seems to be a vicious circle. Order is the remedy, but superficial order breeds more confusion. Although your rational thinking clearly shows you that your nonsensical fears account for your confusion, the analysis itself is not enough for getting out of the confusion. The analysis of your behavior simply shows you what causes your emotional and mental immobilization. But you want more than that. You intuitively know that you want to feel alive, that is, you want to feel your whole self going in the direction that you want to go. You want a rewarding career, a satisfying relationship, or some other goal. You do not want to be pulled in different directions. Endless analysis will not give you this feeling of unity. Only intuition will help you achieve unity in your life. The solution to the problem of eliminating confusion becomes the task of creating a total and vital self. To do this you have to learn how to develop your power of intuition.

Intuition is the innate power of seeing what is ultimately important to you. By the fact that you are aware of your own existence you are potentially aware of all existence. The awareness of your existence is your mental activity cutting through your routine behaviors to see what makes up the heart of your life. You find that you are a center of intellectual and emotional power who can achieve what you want. Besides appreciating yourself you can reach out and enjoy everything which is around you. Each day you miss so much joy because you refuse to shake off your negative attitudes toward yourself. But there are moments in your life when you feel overwhelmed by something or someone extraordinarily beautiful or good. You cannot clearly define what you feel at those moments. But your exclamation such as "Life is good!" is evidence that you have caught a glimpse of what is truly important to you. If you hold on to these moments in your life, you can sharpen your vision of what life means to you.

2. Reflection

Reflecting on your positive feelings of joy and love is the beginning of intuition. Over the years your intuitive knowledge is weakened through acculturation. When you were a child you lived spontaneously, creatively, and joyfully. The social institution of education has undone most of that because it is the vehicle for shaping man according to the demands of society. The boundaries of critical and reflective thinking have been determined by social pressure. If you accept these limitations you will be confused. Limited reflective thinking is a contradiction. To reflect on your life means to think independently. You probably believe that you are doing something wrong if you think differently from social opinion. You are even afraid to face those questions which you feel so deeply. At times you wonder if there is a God, if religion makes sense, if there is such a reality as love, if you honestly love your spouse, and if there is any point to living. You are torn in two directions—you want to answer these questions for yourself, but you are afraid to challenge all the answers that you have learned from your parents, religion and education. Suppose you think through these questions independently and your own answers differ from the ones you have learned. What a frightening thought!

Reflection dispels this confusion. Reflection, that is, raising your mind to an awareness of its past and current positive experiences, prepares you for an insight into the potential of your moral and psychological power.

3. Listening

Listening follows reflection. If you hold your positive experiences within your mind, you will feel the drive for truth and beauty within you. Attentiveness to these movements of consciousness organizes the powers of your whole being to support your attempt to see those realities to which you feel attached. Various types of meditation discipline your senses and mental activities. Through meditation you sharpen your awareness of your internal self. You usually resort to poetic images to explain what you have felt. So you speak of the ocean of calm to express your deep sense of serenity, or you speak of a flash of lightning and a bolt of thunder to describe the suddenness and power of seeing the truth. How often do you say "All of a sudden it struck me"? The "it" could be eternity, death, truth, love, peace, or yourself. But unless you listen you will never see.

Vision then is an awareness of the realities which are important to you. The assumption that there are realities which are not immediately evident to you is proved through your power of intuition. After reflecting and listening to all the realities around you, you eventually look into yourself. You find there a desire for total well-being. You also find powers for achieving a sense of fulfillment. These powers are your will and intellect.

Without the deeper and exalted realities of truth, justice, beauty, and love there is no eros or fire in your daily living. You will tend to generalize particulars, so that all love is in one person, all truth is in one philosophy, all justice is in one political system. When that one love, one philosophy, one social system or one person deceives you, you are confused and disappointed. Only a vision of the powers of your mind and will can restore an abiding order to your life.

The Art of Listening to Yourself

Dialogue 3—Seeing what is important to you

Vision is the power of knowing what is important to you. You experience this power within you in different situations. Reading a powerful novel, walking through the forest, contemplating by the seashore, talking with someone you love, reading an inspiring poem, gazing at a sunset—these are occasions when you clearly see the value of your life. Confusion is the inevitable lot of those who let themselves become mentally flabby. Through mental exercises you can sharpen your memory, reason, and intuition. The clear meaning of your life and the daily enjoyment of feeling alive are the rewards of respecting and using the powers of your mind.

1. Recall a time in your life *when you felt most like yourself.* This experience might have been very simple. For example, you might have been walking through woods, fishing in a lake, talking to a friend, or doing your work. Take a moment to remember the details of that experience.

Briefly describe the time when you felt most like yourself.

What were the deepest feelings you experienced at that time?

What were you saying to yourself at that time?

At that moment what was most important to you?

2. In your mind list five values which are most important to you.

3. Recall what confuses you. For example, I am confused about my relationship with my spouse, boyfriend, or girlfriend. I never seem to be satisfied.

Think about what is important to you. For example, openness and honesty in a relationship are important to me.

Ask yourself if in your relationships you have been acting according to what is important to you. If you have not followed your deep feelings, ask yourself what has been preventing you from doing what is important to you.

Part Two

A MATTER OF CHOICE

4. Hiding

Hiding behind self-sacrifice is a common ploy to avoid self-responsibility. The following story illustrates this point. Linda is a bright young college student living independently in a big city. Although she is financially skimping along with part-time jobs, nevertheless she is generous to her friends and indigent family. Her money problems catch up with her. She is forced to live at home. Within a month she is out on the street because her mother, sisters, and brothers want her out. She drops out of school and temporarily bunks in a dormitory with a girlfriend. Her lot changes when she meets a man holding a steady job. They decide to live together. After several jobs as a supermarket checkout clerk she lands a position with a reputable firm. He sees this turn of events as an opportunity to decide what he really wants to do. For two years Linda subsidizes his career search. In the meantime her realistic goal to return to school and pursue a graduate degree is turning into a fantasy. She justifies her behavior in the name of self-sacrificing love. Somehow, she believes, all her suffering will be rewarded in an everlasting love relationship. In fact, they separated.

The conclusion of this story was inevitable. A relationship built on dependence is doomed from the beginning. Self-sacrifice for Linda was really paying dues for the feeling of security that she experienced in having someone around. Rather than facing her loneliness and then reaching into herself to find security in her own mental and volitional powers, she chose to reach out to seek comfort. To keep this comfort, she gave up herself. But this kind of self-sacrifice is neither noble nor altruistic. It is emotional suicide. Behavior of this sort is motivated by having comfort and security which comes in many forms—money, affection, or prestige. True self-sacrifice, authentic altruism, or love is based on loving yourself. But loving oneself is being and not having. To be oneself is to exercise your highest faculties for your own good. You use your mind to see yourself honestly—that is, to know your powers, your destiny and your meaning. You use your will to choose the values and the actions which will strengthen your freedom. When your current of life—your mind and your will—is constantly expanding, then love is possible because you can give. However, when you choose to be dependent, you dam your stream of life. There is nothing to give but stagnating water.

The route to dependence is often your escape from confusion. You experience mental fatigue when you face the same problems. Because you consider yourself unequal to the task, you search for answers outside yourself.

Fundamental questions such as "Who am I?" and "Why am I alive?" grip your attention in your quiet moments. At a time like this you feel far removed from the sea of humanity. Suddenly you recognize that you are an individual who is different from everyone else. In your loneliness, the question "Who am I?" resounds with greater force. Because you feel apart from everyone, you can only find the answer to the question of your identity by yourself within your solitude. The responsibility for a definite answer to the question "Who am I?" is clearly yours and only yours. But if you are afraid to be alone, you could pass through life as a stranger to yourself.

Life becomes a contradiction without a definition of yourself. You fill the world with words, but within you are silent. You have answers to everybody's problems, but you are afraid to face your own questions. You fill each day with enough activity to keep the "Who am I?" question in the backwaters of your mind. But constant distraction does not put the question to rest.

To assuage the feeling of drifting into loneliness you seek the attachment of the people around you. Their reassuring comments will make you feel accepted. You prefer to have these people tell you who you are. As long as you behave according to their wishes you know that you will receive their approval. When you are approved, then you know that you have measured up to someone else's idea about who you are. The true answer to your question "Who am I?" is never really made. However, the symptomatic pain of confusion and loneliness is relieved because in being approved you no longer feel apart. You trade the pain of confusion for the pain of anxiety. Now you worry about keeping the attachments upon which you depend so much for your feeling of security. You know that your fragile comfort can be easily shattered by the capriciousness of other human beings. With one wrong move you can lose the approval of a parent, a teacher, a spouse, a lover, or a boss.

Measuring up to an image of what you are supposed to be is another unproductive external way of answering the fundamental internal question of "Who am I?" This way of thinking is different from approval seeking because you are not afraid to be alone. Although you are relying on external sources to answer the "Who am I?" question, nevertheless you do not seek the approval of these sources, which could be people, an ideology, a religion, or popular social opinions. The method is external because outside sources account for the content of the image of yourself. Although the process of constructing an idea of yourself takes place within your own mind, you look for the building materials outside your mind. For example, from your youth you may have been modeling your behavior on an ideal image of yourself based on a religion, a philosophy, or a hero. The meaning of your life became dependent on the actualization of that particular image. If you have lived this way, you probably experienced several positive results. For one thing behaving according to a model substituted order for confusion. Living according to a blueprint also gave you a feeling of success because you could clearly check your progress. However, as you grew intellectually, you probably outgrew your ideal self-image. Your understanding at age eighteen of the perfect Christian, Jew, Muslim, parent, lover, or spouse was different from your understanding of that person ten years later.

The pain of confusion recurs as long as you behave without a true knowledge of yourself. When you act to win approval, you will behave inconsistently because there are too many variables to manage. Living your life according to other people's expectations becomes an exercise in play acting. When your theatre is the day-to-day world around you, you cannot control the mood of the audience. Instead, *you* are controlled by everyone passing before you. You run into insoluble difficulties with this condescending attitude. If you need approval for meaning, then you need it from everyone around you. But how can you please everyone equally—your husband and your mother, your boss and your peers, your children and your grandchildren, or your nephews and nieces, without displeasing someone?

Because you assume that the answers to the fundamental questions of your existence are in sources outside yourself, the irrational tendency of dependence takes hold of your life. When you believe that the answers to life are "out there," you deprive yourself of internal rational discourse which is your most vital activity. *Self stroking.*

Looking down on yourself

If you feel that you are a dependent person, then you probably feel inferior to other people in most situations. You are always looking up to another person or group of people whom you slavishly admire. But in fact you are not small. You appear little to yourself because you magnify the attractive qualities of other people. Then you compare your weaknesses to their strengths. The perfection of these heroes is the product of your romantic thinking. What you are really doing is comparing yourself to the way that you would like to be with the way you are. Because the gap is so wide between the two images, you begin to feel disappointed with yourself.

To avoid the feeling of weakness caused by dependence, you mask your sense of inferiority with the idea of loyalty. The feeling of strength flowing from your blind commitment to another person or group of persons justifies your refusal to think independently. You attempt to escape the covert feelings of inferiority by identifying yourself with a person whom you believe to be strong. Your strength is tied to this person's success. However, the camouflaged feelings of your own worthlessness persistently taunt you. They emerge with all their fury whenever your hero fails. For example, when outstanding political or religious leaders slip in popularity their dependent followers are thrown into mental and emotional confusion. To escape their pain they look for new heroes.

Other people prefer to escape their feelings of insecurity about their own worth by totally submerging themselves in the work of an organization. Each moment is devoted to the business of the company, the church, the professional organization, or the cause. Unless some people are actively attached to an institution they feel worthless. But the inordinate desire to be connected to a conventional organization is tantamount to saying that they derive their meaning from a social institution. By comparing their rather small roles to the grandiose goals of the institution they silently admit that they are inferior. But they camouflage their self-debasement by hiding in the shadows of the organization's leaders.

If you invest your heroes and institutions with an ideal perfection, then your behavior toward the authorities of those institutions becomes unduly deferential. You begin to identify the ideal perfection of the institution with the leaders of the institution. After having performed this marriage, you then commit your loyalty to these authorities in order to escape the barrenness of your own existence. The desire to revere and respect life is so great that if you do not accept your own self-worth you will fabricate an ideal reality to venerate.

The predominant behavior of the dependent person is approval-seeking. If you are always trying to please others to receive their approbation, then you are dependent on approval to feel good about yourself. If you are neglected by significant people in your life, you feel that you are nobody. The eyes of others subtly control your behavior. Softly and almost imperceptibly you ask yourself before each action, "Who is looking?"

When your feeling of worth depends on approval, then arbitrary matters such as a high grade on a test, a good word from the boss, the applause of the crowd, a big sale, or a reassuring word from your spouse become very important to you. If you don't receive this approval you quickly plunge yourself into the murky waters of depression. I'm not ok

If you are a dependent person you are probably anxious. The sense of an impending loss lurks behind your thinking and behaviors. You believe that you are the prey. You feel the sights of someone's wrath trained on your very existence. You can almost smell the smoke of your own destruction. The aggressor could be anyone of several people. The time could be any occasion. The place could be anywhere. You must constantly be on your guard. Against what, you do not know. To protect what, you do not truly know.

Because you have become dependent on someone, some idea, or some organization for your self-worth, you have become extremely vulnerable. Your life is tenuously dangling from the thread of approval. If someone cuts it, "all" is lost. However, you really do not know what the "all" is, because you never understood the basis for your self-worth in the first place. You know there is some relationship between your life and worth. Because you are unclear about the nature of this relationship you can easily think that your life will be ruined if what you depend on for worth is lost. You clearly do not have control over your happiness when you have centered the meaning of your life in someone or something outside yourself. Consequently, you are gripped by anxiety, because you might be a big zero if you lose a career, if you fail in a relationship, if you are fired, or if you challenge authority and lose.

Anger is another feeling which can be traced to dependence. When you demand perfection of yourself, you put your worth on the line of performance. You see yourself being destroyed as you make mistakes. If you do not succeed according to your self-imposed standards you become violent and abusive toward yourself or toward the people obstructing your flawless performance. You use force to destroy whatever is preventing your success. The tactics you use may be passive or active. For example, in a work situation you will withhold information from your co-workers because giving them additional knowledge will make them more competitive. Then your success will be threatened by their success. On the other hand your success may depend on someone else's performance. Then you become verbally aggressive toward these people when they slough off. In both instances you feel anger because your success is threatened.

If you are a dependent person you are followed by the shadow of guilt. You fear that you have done something wrong or that you might cross someone. Since your life is guided by the ideas of unquestioned loyalty and approval, you enormously increase the probability of perceiving yourself doing something wrong. You always feel guilty for not knowing what is expected of you. Consequently, you feel ashamed because you assume the responsibility of foreseeing what someone expects of you. How often have you said "I should have known what he wanted"? Doesn't the loyal employee try to anticipate his superior's actions? Doesn't the perfect secretary do the little extras which are more than required? And if she does not cater to the boss's idiosyncrasies, does she not scold herself for not knowing what she should know? Before long you feel yourself losing control because you see too many things expected of you by too many people. You cannot keep up with the demands that you foresee, so you break down. Then you finish yourself off with a final blow when you tell yourself that you are bad because you cannot fulfill all these fictitious demands. Women who are mothers often experience this type of guilt, because they feel that there should be more to being a mother than what they are doing. Men who are fathers experience the same guilt. Mothers and fathers search in vain for the secrets of being perfect parents.

Besides feeling guilty for not knowing what you think you should know, you feel guilty when your performance falls short of some external standard. For example, you may have failed to satisfy the goals which your parents had for you, or you may have missed the mark in gaining your boss's approval. If you review your actions carefully, you will see that you learned these feelings of guilt from early childhood. When you were forced as a child to compete in academics, sports, and affection, you learned that success depended on the approval of the people important to you. You learned to identify acceptance of yourself with approval. But competition by its very nature allows outstanding success to a small percentage of the people. Consequently, you feel mediocre about yourself because you never excelled in school, in sports, in work, or in the arts. You think of yourself as getting by. In your mature years you readily experience guilt because you feel that you never are all that you should be. Getting by is no longer a satisfying philosophy of life.

Your dissatisfaction with yourself degenerates into blaming behaviors. In a marital crisis you usually focus on deficiencies. You blame either yourself or your partner for your dissatisfaction. Then each of you promptly feels guilty for what you have done to the other. You try to change your negative behavior to return to the good graces of the other. The ensuing pleasant moments deceive you. What you think is a bond of love is a bond of guilt. Your responses were cued by your pangs of guilt instead of your honest feeling to know yourself and your spouse in spite of each other's weaknesses. Rather than confront yourself and your spouse, you prefer to behave cautiously to avoid future incidents. By behaving this way you immobilize yourself by twisting your mind into one big knot. For example, you tell yourself that you are discontented with your marriage, but there is not much you can do. When you have reached your limit of dissatisfaction you complain and blame. Then you feel guilty for having behaved so deplorably. To make amends you shower your spouse with affection. Before long you find yourself going through the same pattern, but the feelings of guilt and dissatisfaction become more acute. Eventually, you cannot sustain the pain of being confused so you look for escape routes. Some of your unsuccessful attempts to alleviate your pain are sleep, drugs, and apathy. None of these works. You have failed to see the real cause of your dissatisfaction which is the real guilt of not accepting responsibility for your own feelings.

Authentic guilt is the feeling of emptiness which you have brought on yourself. You are empty because you have chosen not to initiate your own actions. You choose to avoid responsibility. Real guilt means that you cannot give yourself any excuses for the way you behave. Making mistakes and not receiving approval do not constitute authentic guilt. When you experience real guilt, that is, the recognition of your own omission to decide what you want to do, then you begin to behave responsibly. Real guilt does not last long.

Two ways of thinking which keep you dependent

1. Dogmatism and dependence

The ineffective behaviors and feelings associated with dependence are caused by the rigid thinking styles of dogmatism and romanticism. Dogmatic thinking bases itself on unquestioned assumptions about reality. When you are confused, you know that you need a definite system of thought which will give sense to your life. The feeling of frustration arising from apparent contradictions prepares you to accept a ready-made system of thought which you believe will put your mind in order. Dogmas and teachings give you a theoretical system for putting realities in place. For example, death makes sense if you know that there is life after death. Obedience to law makes sense if you know that one day you will be rewarded. Love makes sense if we know that you will be loved in return. All the complexities of life and all the existential contradictions are resolved by dogmatism. Acceptance of the dogma frees you from being immobilized by confusion. Your task is to apply the dogmas to your daily life. This type of thinking satisfies your desire for mental comfort. You feel sure of your behaviors because you know that your actions are sanctioned by long-established teachings of a reputable religion or ideology.

However, dogmatic thinking with all its do's and don't's never successfully gives you the meaning of life. The reality underlying the dogma forces changes in your belief systems. Within the last few years of your life you probably have experienced these changes. Even the dogmas and practices of institutions change, but you want no change. You believe that your rigid adherence to former dogmas will continue to give meaning to your life. Ironically, it is this very rigidity of thought that fills you with anger and anxiety. In the presence of change you feel that you must remain loyal to these teachings or else you will suffer unbearable guilt. By adhering blindly to absolute dogmas you will once again suffer the pain of confusion.

Your dogmas may be inconsistent with the demands you feel within yourself to broaden your view of life. You intuitively feel that your life is more than what you currently think about it. But you are afraid to challenge the ideas which you were taught and by which you have lived so long. You fear that you will be left with nothing if you cast aside a way of life which has served you so well. Yet you persistently feel the push to expand your vision of yourself. So you are caught in a dilemma. Do you play it safe and identify your life with your ideas about life, or do you venture to shape new ideas about life based on what you intuitively know?

2. Romanticism

Romanticism is a belief about the way the world should be. Since the world is not the way it should be, you reject it. What you do accept is your own ideas. You then construct an ideal world with your own thoughts. Your new system of thought becomes your ideology, that is, the pattern of ideas guiding your actions. Your feelings and behaviors become dependent on it. However, you soon experience the contradictions between your ideal world and the world you daily encounter. Your ideal world turns out to be words. You have constructed a pattern of ideas which has no reference to the world you experience. Rather than suffer this pain of contradiction you withdraw to your own world.

Fusing the ideal with the real is a common problem. How often are you disillusioned when you have not found the ideal husband or wife? How often do you feel guilty because you do not behave the way your ideal self would? How often are you angry because humans do not behave ideally? How often are you anxious when you can no longer ignore the unpredictability of reality? You will feel anxious, angry and confused unless you substitute your rigid thinking styles with types of thinking which are in tune with your deep commonsense feelings about the meaning of your life.

Something to think about

Do you think about yourself as someone whose needs must be satisfied?

Or

Do you think about yourself as someone who sees values and acts on them?

If you see yourself as someone "needing," then you probably feel dependent most of the time.

If you see yourself as someone "valuing," then you probably feel independent most of the time. When you are valuing, you are judging how, when, and where you can do what is important to you.

To understand the difference between these two ways of seeing yourself, use love as an example. The "needing" you means that you *must* receive affection, attention, and caring. The "valuing" you means that you *want to give* affection, attention, and caring. To appreciate the difference more vividly, act out your valuing self for three days. At the end of this period review the feelings that you were experiencing. Did you feel more in control of yourself?

The Art of Listening to Yourself

Dialogue 4—Spotting your irrational dependencies

When a person throws up his hands in surrender, he lets his captor take complete charge of him. People who give up under stress and confusion turn their minds over to someone or something. They become dependent on physical comforts such as drugs, the mental escapes of fantasies, and blind personal attachments. Their minds are in the bondage of ignorance. When they quit the struggle to search for a meaningful life, they give up their freedom to do what is important to them. Now they do what their irrational dependencies tell them to do. Like all prisoners they have little responsibility and little happiness.

1. Discover the tyrant in your life by reviewing the statements that you make to yourself. This exercise requires attention, because there can be a thin line between irrational dependencies and fruitful desires. For example, I desire a good meal, but if it is burnt, I can survive without going into a rage. Or I want a promotion, but I'm not wiped out if I don't get it.

   By examining the statements that you make to yourself, you can discover your irrational dependencies. For example, in your relationships you might be quietly telling yourself that you abso-lutely need this person's attention, and if you do not receive the recognition that you demand, you will feel bad about yourself.

Which of the following statements do you usually make to yourself? If no statement in the list applies to you, think about the absolute demands that you ordinarily make upon yourself and/ or others.

_____I must succeed at everything I do.
_____I must always be right.
_____I must be approved by everyone.
_____I must be 100% sure before I do anything.
_____Without my fantasies I could not live.
_____I can't stand feeling anxious.
_____I must be perfect.
_____I must have the comfort of _____.
_____I cannot stand friction in a relationship.

2. When your dependencies are not satisfied how do you feel? Use the following statement as a model to clarify your feelings. When my dependency for *getting attention is not satisfied*, I feel *depressed*.

5. A Tight Grip on the Reins

The manager of a large business worries from time to time about losing control over his personnel, his share of the market, and countless details which hold an operation together. Working as a college administrator, I observed the strange behaviors of presidents and deans who feared losing control of the faculty, the student body, and their sources of information such as middle management administrators and secretaries. I recall one dean who was possessed with the passion of scrupulously monitoring the recording of grades. At the end of each semester the instructor was required to report his or her grades on three grade sheets, one for the computer center, one for the dean's office, and one for the instructor. A secretary would check the office copy against the computer copy before sending the grades to the computer center. The computer center recorded the grades on the students' transcripts. The dean's office received two copies of each student's transcript. The computer center also sent the dean a verification grade list for each course given during the semester which reported the grade of each student in the course. The students were informed of their grades by mail. They received individual notices for each grade. The dean's office was sent a copy of each grade notice sent to the students. These notices, amounting to approximately 35,000 each semester, were then alphabetized by a clerk in the dean's office. Each student's transcript was then microfilmed and stored in the basement. At the end of this tedious operation one grade was recorded twelve times. Of course, the lion's share was in the dean's office.

One day the dean was rushed off to the hospital. Diagnosis: hypertension. Ironically, he had lost control of himself.

Internal positive control

Positive control is internal. You can achieve mastery of your negative feelings by rationally ordering your thoughts. Falling apart or losing control is your personal responsibility. The ensuing pain of confusion is the result of surrendering your power of reason. If you recognize that you have caused your own mental confusion, you are well on the way to restoring mental order.

When you have achieved a good measure of internal control you feel superior to the forces in any situation. You are no longer bullied into confusion by intimidating people. Challenging situations such as examinations, interviews, sales encounters, or personal encounters no longer threaten you. You can accept your own emotional and intellectual limitations without being depressed. Your realistic view of the world and of yourself constantly contributes to your power of control. By accepting yourself as you are and the world as it is, you put yourself in a favorable position to analyze your problem accurately and calmly. You no longer frantically try to force people and events into the ways that you think that they should be. You simply accept them the way they are. You realize that your difficulties are solved by changing your thinking and not by changing the behavior of others.

You feel powerful because you are growing in knowledge of yourself. Where you were timid, now you are bold. Where you were apologetic, now you are assertive. Where you were uncertain, now you are sure. Where you were anxious, now you are confident. You see yourself as an adult capable of solving your own problems.

Negative control

Negative control is attempting to manage events and people around you by using defensive behaviors. If your emotional stability and overall sense of well-being depend on the actions of others, then anyone can pose a threat to you. You must be on your guard to ward off the demeaning word or the aggressive behavior which may come from any quarter. Since the best defense is a good offense, you make up your mind to be aggressive in word and action. By keeping everyone off balance you can more easily control their behavior. However, because you do not want to incite rebellion in other people, your aggressiveness is tempered by prudence. Unruly behavior on the part of others will jeopardize the control that you eagerly desire.

You can frequently behave this way when you are in a position of authority. At work in a large company or institution, you can manage the behaviors of other people by raising and lowering their anxiety levels. You are probably being managed the same way by someone else. Nevertheless, if you can control the people and events around you, you believe that you will have strengthened your own position. In your mind the mark of power and success is control.

The danger of control

As I mentioned above, the power of the idea of order can contribute to your growth or maintain your mediocrity. If order and control combine to protect what you have, then living becomes a routine of possessing. The deeper realities of liberty and creativity are never keenly experienced. The spontaneity and freedom of love threaten you because you fear you might lose what you possess. How often have you refused to be involved in issues concerning justice because you feared retaliation? How often have you rationalized your silence by arguing that you cannot beat the system? How often have you told yourself that when you are in a position of authority you will rectify the injustices. Now it is better to hold your peace so that you do not minimize your chance for that higher position. There are so many excuses for escaping the responsibility of behaving freely.

The feeling of security reinforces your desire for control. When your world is stable your chances of experiencing the pain of confusion are minimal. As long as the external world conforms to your ideas of it, you can predict your own behavior as well as the behavior of others. No evil can befall you because you believe that you control the forces accounting for your well-being. You feel confident that you can protect what you have. Your land, your money, your reputation and your children are tightly in your grasp.

When you persist in trying to control the world around you, you begin to feel anxious. Knowing that the world does not exactly fit your ideas of it you feel that events, people, and things are slipping from your grasp. The more they elude your hold, the more impetuously you try to corral them. For example, as your children psychologically distance themselves from you, you become more concerned that you might lose them. Your irrational belief that you can control their love for you is challenged. Instead of giving up this belief, you behave more irrationally out of your feelings of anxiety. You sense that your world will fall apart if they adopt values different from your own. What you worked so hard and so long to possess is being lost. The tragedy of this type of anxiety is the fact that love is not a possession in the first place. What you thought was love was something else. You do not lose love. You decide not to love. Love is a personal act and not a possession.

Only an internal security rooted in the power of choosing the type of person you want to be can minimize your feelings of anxiety. No person, no event, or no thing can threaten you from being who you want to be. True interior control then is based on your vision of what a human being is and on your vision of what it takes to be the person you want to be. When you choose to behave according to the human values that you see, then you can achieve internal control of your feelings.

Thinking legally

Legal thinking dominates the mental processes of the person desiring control over himself and others. You have learned from early childhood that law is a power which directs your behavior. Rarely have you understood the source and the mechanics of law. However, you know that punishment is the consequence of disobeying the law. Over the years you have connected law with authority, authority with power, and power with control. Once you are convinced that law shapes human behavior, then you begin to use the authority and power of your reason to construct laws which will bring about the types of behavior you want for yourself and others. For example, some marriages are built around a legal statement. The partners write out the do's and don't's that will guide each other's behavior in the marriage.

When you attempt to make your behavior totally dependent on law, then you have arrived at the point where you are controlled by the idea of control. Your reason is performing its operations to construct a system of do's and don't's which will control your behavior. The assumption underlying this process states that obedience to regulations will maximize the feeling of satisfaction. Consequently, you will minimize the pain of anxiety derived from being uncertain. However, when you make your reason subordinate to the idea of control, you become irrational. The object of reason is truth and understanding, not blind loyalty to rules.

The process by which you achieve productive control is different from control. You achieve rational control of your feelings and behavior through the *free* exercise of reason. It is absurd to think that you can take charge of your behaviors and feelings by limiting your thinking. Although you make laws for yourself to guide your behaviors, nevertheless you will feel obliged at times to change these laws. For example, you may have told yourself that your profession is always number one in your life. All your behaviors are motivated by advancement in your career. However, your love for another person can challenge the absolute importance that you give to your career. If your obsessive adherence to your laws prevents you from discovering more about life, then you will never understand the law of love which says, "Open up to life and trust it."

You assume your tendency to control has supremacy over your tendencies to understand and to be free. This assumption is unfounded, because true order and true control contribute to feeling and behaving spontaneously and creatively. Control for the sake of avoiding uncertainty is a denial of life.

When your thinking is going against the grain of your deep common-sense feelings about life, then you experience conflicts among your thinking, feeling, and behavior. You intuitively feel that life is expansive, novel, enjoyable, creative, free, powerful, and communicative. Using the idea of control to escape your own freedom and that of others generates feelings of rebellion or regret. If you intensely want to feel the joys and sorrows of life, you will abruptly rid yourself of your rigid regulations.

The Art of Listening to Yourself

Dialogue 5—Who's controlling whom?

The feeling of being all together is the result of being in control of your life. When you see what you want to do and you have the power to do it, then you experience control. You see what is important to you in a concrete situation; then you guide your ideas, feelings, and behaviors accordingly. Only a deep understanding of what you are doing and why you are doing it can give you a feeling of true control. Even if the order attached to your activity as mother, father, spouse, or worker, guides your day-to-day life, you are not in control of yourself unless you choose to put your personal values in these activities.

1. In the following activities do you feel controlled or free? If you do not feel like yourself in an activity, review your behaviors and irrational dependencies to discover what is controlling you.

   Parent
   Spouse
   Lover
   Worker
   Friend
   Daughter
   Son
   Student

2. Complete each sentence that applies to you.

   When people at work do not do what I tell them, I lose control of myself because . . .

When my children do not do what I tell them, I lose control of myself because . . .

When my boyfriend/girlfriend behaves openly and spontaneously, I feel that I might lose control of myself because . . .

When I do not finish what I planned to do in a day, I lose control of myself because . . .

When people close to me do not show their appreciation for me, I lose control of myself because . . .

When my boss criticizes me, I lose control of myself because . . .

When my work goes unnoticed, I lose control of myself because . . .

3. Look closely at the reasons you gave for being upset. If you lose control of yourself because people do not do what you think they should do, then you are allowing other people to control you. People can and will behave unpleasantly toward you, but that is no reason for getting upset. Instead of focusing your attention on what other people *should* do and think, concentrate on what *you want* to do and think.

4. Change each of the above incomplete sentences around to read the following one:

Because (independence, rationality . . .) is important to me, when people at work do not do what I tell them, then I will . . .

5. When you find yourself in one of those "upsetting" situations, begin reflecting by saying to yourself, "Because _____ is important to me . . ."

6. The Courage to Choose

Jim was in his late twenties. He was single and constantly looking for that perfect mate. Every romantic relationship was painful for him because he suffered from "incurable jealousy." The view that he had of himself was someone who needed to have his ideal woman. The perceptions he had of the women in his relationships were very much affected by the way he saw himself. In each relationship the woman became the object he had to have. He complained that he never felt free with a woman because he spent most of his time thinking of ways to control her. Each time that he failed, he became angry. The following dialogue gets at the heart of the matter.

Jim: I can't understand what's going on. The beginning of this relationship was great. Now the same thing that happened in all the others is happening again.
Counselor: What thing is happening again, Jim?
Jim: In the beginning it was just ourselves doing everything together. Now, she starts to do things on her own.
Counselor: Like what?
Jim: Well, for example, last Saturday she took a trip to the country without telling *me* about it first.
Counselor: You sound as if you are angry about that.
Jim: Yes, damn it. She should have told me.

Counselor: Because . . .

Jim: Because she is mine.

Counselor: You seem to believe that you own her.

Jim: Well, I *really* don't own her. It's just that I need her.

Counselor: You see yourself as needing her very much.

Jim: I've always seen myself as someone looking for that perfect woman. Somehow I feel incomplete until I can have her.

Counselor: But each time that you find her what happens?

Jim: After a while I begin to feel miserable. I don't feel free. I get angry easily. Then I'm down on myself.

Counselor: What are you saying to yourself when you feel this way?

Jim: I can never seem to get what I want in a relationship.

Counselor: And what do you want?

Jim: I want to feel free and happy.

Counselor: And how do you think she wants to feel?

Jim: The same way, I guess.

Counselor: If she wants to feel free and happy how do you think you might view her?

Jim: Well, I guess I could see her as someone who is free to be happy.

Counselor: And how might you see yourself?

Jim: I could see myself the same way.

Counselor: If you saw yourself as someone who is free to do what is important for yourself, how do you think that you would feel toward your girlfriend?

Jim: I would no longer feel that I needed her, but then I would not feel certain about her. I mean . . . maybe I wouldn't be able to hold on to her.

Counselor: Have you been able to hold on to the others?

Jim: No.

Counselor: What would the consequences be for you if you stopped seeing yourself as someone who *needed* your ideal woman?

Jim: I would feel much more free.

Counselor: But yet you still want a close relationship with a woman. What would be the consequences if you saw yourself as someone who is free to give attention, concern, and care to a woman?

When Jim consciously changed his view of himself from some-one who needed to someone who is free to give, he began to see the woman in his life differently. Also, he behaved and felt differently.

The yearning to be free

Day after day you long to be free from your daily routine. The belief that one day all this boredom will be behind you gives you the minimum amount of strength to get up in the morning and to do the things expected of you.

Popularly, feeling free means that you do not want to be told what to do, you do not want to be forced to work at uninteresting jobs, you do not want to be financially dependent on someone else, and you do not want your thinking to be controlled. When you look closely at the things that you don't want, you see clearly that this type of freedom means escape from life. You are caught in the contradiction of making your feeling of freedom dependent on either the perfection or the elimination of the realities of life. Living this contradiction is the feeling of being pulled in opposite directions. You want to be responsible to your obligations, and you want to enjoy the passion of living. You want to be realistic and idealistic at the same time. Your body goes through the motions demanded by your routine, but your mind is somewhere else. This false idea of freedom reduces the possible feeling of freedom to an unrealizable hope. Your life becomes a continual belief in something you never feel.

Your life becomes boring. Boredom is marking time, monotony, routine, and sameness. However, the recurrence of events is not the essence of boredom. Everyday there is sunrise and a sunset, but we can hardly say that these phenomena are monotonous. The surgeon may routinely perform a serious operation a hundred times, but the hundred and first time is not necessarily boring. The therapist may be working with the problem of depression for the hundredth time, but he or she does not necessarily become depressed because of the repitition. Boredom occurs when you relax your mind and will. You search for comfort instead of challenge. You let yourself be carried along by the rhythm of events instead of directing events according to the rhythm of your own mind.

Your own will and mind are the sources of the novelty and the spontaneity in your life. These are the centers of your creative energies and your freedom. Feeling free comes when you commit your mind and will to see and respond to the creative energy within yourself and others. Freedom is not escape. Freedom is creative responsibility.

When you feel free you accept the responsibility for your behaviors and feelings. There is little room for blaming and complaining. Your sense of responsibility brands your actions and feelings with your identity. If you are feeling angry, you do not say, "They make me angry." If you feel depressed, you do not say, "The world is evil." If you feel lonely, you do not say, "No one understands me." And you do not say, "People make me feel guilty." Feeling angry is my anger. Feeling depressed is my depression. Likewise, feeling joy is my joy. Knowing that your feelings and behaviors have their roots in your mind and will, you can feel free even if those feelings and behaviors are negative. You see yourself as the cause of your own problems. This view of yourself as a center of action prevents you from lapsing into dependency. You begin to see that you can control yourself and your social environment. When you stop to think what your mind can contain, you are amazed by its power. The human tragedy is not to use it.

Having been convinced of your ability to understand yourself, you accept the responsibility for putting meaning in your life. The purpose of living is to do. Living becomes meaningful when you choose to direct your mind to see the beginning and the end of your life. The beginning is ignorance and dependence. The end is wisdom and freedom. After choosing your goal according to your basic values you use the knowledge that you have of yourself and the world to decide on meaningful actions. Then you move to achieve those goals. The feeling of freedom comes when you apply your efforts to do those things which express your values.

Seeing yourself free and seeing yourself realistically go together. You cannot be free without being realistic, nor can you be realistic without being free. You recognize your own deficiencies as well as those of the people around you. You take obstacles and failures for granted, but they do not discourage you. Those who think they can never do what they want because circumstances and people are against them will never feel free. To be free is to be real.

And to be free is to suffer discomfort. To be subservient is unreal. And to be subservient is to avoid discomfort.

When you get a taste of freedom you become sharply aware that the power to grow in all aspects of your life is within you. For the greater part of your life these enormous reserves of mental and volitional energies go untapped. If you have been brought up on the pabulum of dependency, you feel powerless to do what you want because you do not act until you have someone's approval or encouragement to go ahead. The feelings of spontaneity, enthusiasm, and confidence so evident in children are stifled as you grow older. You must regain the childlike feeling of freedom to dispel all your "if only" irrational beliefs, such as: If only I had been born ten years earlier when there was a booming job market, if only I had married someone with more money, etc. The reality of life is that the now moment is the only moment for you. Your power is in seizing the moment to do what you want now.

Just as the idea of freedom prepares you to accept and want yourself, so also it helps you to respect others. However, your interest in others does not blind you to their negative behaviors and feelings. As a free person you feel powerful to reject their repressive behaviors even if they belong to someone very close to you. Dependent people would rather find excuses for someone's nonsensical behavior than reject it. By being critical you run the risk of losing someone's approval. But if you support the irrational behaviors of others, in the long run they lose their respect for you. People whose relationships are guided by freedom accept each other unconditionally. Their love is real.

When you act freely your behaviors are strong and determined. You clearly see the goal that you want to achieve. You are fully aware that you are responsible for its accomplishment. However, your attitude of independence does not prevent you from taking counsel from wise and experienced people. You do not undermine your sense of independence by seeking advice in important matters. The process of arriving at a course of action involves communicating with people who are able to help you foresee the consequences of your contemplated action. Once you have concluded the investigative stages, then you accept full responsibility for deciding on a particular course of action.

In acting freely, you act decisively. Your will is one hundred percent behind the course of action that you have mapped out. You act enthusiastically. All your mental and physical powers converge on your faculty of perception. You do what you want to do with deep feeling.

When you behave decisively and enthusiastically in interpersonal relationships, you experience this concrete freedom. You can love another person only when you act out of an understanding of your own personal goals, out of a sense of independence, out of affirmation for yourself, and finally out of responsibility. You are in effect saying to the other person in your behavior, "This is me, and I want you to want me." When two people behave this way, love is possible because both are making themselves transparent. They can respond to each other authentically and with trust. However, when you camouflage yourself by behaving out of dependence, fear, or anxiety, then love is not a reality.

Behaving freely is difficult, and doing something difficult requires courage. Love demands that you be your true self. And being your true self means being free. When you are no longer dependent on someone's approval, someone's idea of what you should be, or some romantic idea of yourself, then you are able to create yourself through the power of your own will and intellect. The task of becoming yourself through the power of your own activity is arduous, because you are forcing yourself to go beyond the status quo. Usually, human existence is arranged conveniently for you. Life can be a series of roles which you perform. If you dare to become yourself by rewriting the script to fit your personal goals, you run the risk of rejection and discomfort. Rather than lose approval and comfort you rationalize yourself into believing that your happiness and freedom consist in having the rewards of being dependent. In the end you become a psychological prisoner of your dependencies. To be truly free is to be. To be demands that you courageously look into yourself and accept what you find.

Joy is the ebullient sensation that you experience when you know that you are in charge of yourself. You have no fear of losing yourself. The opposite of joy is depression. The greatest misery that you can suffer is the complete psychological loss of self. When you possess yourself you no longer fear that someone might rob you of your happiness. You are joyful because you have chosen to be yourself. Joy is the reward of being free and courageous.

Freedom and introspection

Freedom is an idea described richly over the centuries; nevertheless you do not grasp its concreteness in an idea. Freedom is experienced when you remind yourself that the action you are performing is the one you want to do. You are the center of your actions. You are so powerful that you can initiate or stop your own mental activities provided you want to accept the consequences of your decisions. For example, if I want to write I can do so; if I want to stop writing I can do so. When you reflect on yourself in this manner, you are looking into yourself to find the beginnings of your external behaviors. Reflecting within yourself on yourself as an aware and active being is introspection. By thinking of yourself in this manner you see that you are a center of mental and emotional energies capable of realizing numerous possibilities. It is not far-fetched to say that you can become what you want. Introspection feeds the fires of motivation. You see the gap between what you are doing and what you want to do. Through introspection you see that the center of your being is your awareness of yourself as a free doer. When you allow yourself to become a forced doer, then you surrender yourself to whatever is forcing you. Only lack of courage prevents you from being what you want to be.

Habit and conditioning are two types of human behavior which can smother your self-awareness and, consequently, your freedom. Through conditioning you develop a habit of responding uniformly and almost automatically in given situations. Your answer to the question "Who am I?" is "I am what I do." However, this type of thinking does not explain why you do what you do. For example, a woman may be conditioned to behave as a typical housewife without understanding why she behaves this way. If she searches for her meaning as a human being, she may eventually choose to behave differently. By deepening her thoughts about herself she will arrive at a level of awareness in which she sees herself as a choosing being.

When you are present to yourself, your perceptions of the

world are enriched. External realities no longer appear as ghostly shadows. The more you are in touch with yourself, the more you are struck by people's uniqueness. Because your center of consciousness extends itself through your body, you are more sympathetic to the richness of the realities you perceive.

Without a deep consciousness of self it is difficult to discern value. The more you function out of routine and habit, the more you perceive the world homogeneously. In the end you lose your power to discriminate. You can no longer see what is important. The devaluation of life comes with the loss of personal consciousness. Introspection is the safeguard for your own personal value and the value of others.

The Art of Listening to Yourself

Dialogue 6—Deciding to do what is important to you

The essence of freedom is the action of a person searching for values, choosing values and ultimately practicing values. Freedom, then, is the energy that we spend in pushing our minds to see the meaning of life. When we live according to what we see, then our freedom is complete. Only the free person experiences a passionate love for life.

1. Recall the five values which are most important to you; then think of specific behaviors of putting them into practice. For example: Because independence of mind and a promotion are important to me, I will clearly and confidently express my ideas and feelings concerning my performance at work to my supervisor.

2. Rehearse your behaviors.

   Think of a situation in which you usually feel anxious—for example, presenting your reasons for a promotion; meeting someone for the first time; talking before a large group of people;

being assertive with an authority figure; being romantic with someone you like, etc.

Visualize yourself as a confident, calm, and courageous person who knows and does what is important.

Imagine yourself in the anxiety-provoking situation.

See yourself choosing your words and behaviors according to what is most important to you in that situation.

See yourself behaving in the ways that you have chosen.

In reality, choose the time and place when and where you will actually do what you rehearsed in your imagination. For example: If you have difficulty meeting people for the first time, begin a conversation with someone at your next class, your next stop at the bar, or on the bus.

Part Three

UPS AND DOWNS
IN THE FLOW OF LIFE

7. Bucking Your Dependencies

In the spring of 1968 I was on my way for dinner at the university cafeteria in Paris. As I crossed Boulevard Raspail I froze in my tracks when I saw a throng of humanity surging toward me. Thousands of students locked arm in arm and cordoned by a human rope on each flank chanted their slogans for social, political, and economic reform. The student revolution of 1968 was on. For the next two months Paris and other major cities in France were paralyzed by droves of rebellious students taking over public buildings, burning cars, and digging up the cobblestones to fling at society's symbol of authority, the policemen. The government passed off the student uprising as one of those spring rituals until the workers began siding up with the student leaders. Within a few weeks France was shut down by a general strike. Everything, including the electricity, stopped. The government was on the verge of collapse.

Late one evening I was strolling down Rue de Rennes toward my apartment when I spotted some commotion in the distance. I picked up my pace. At the intersection of Rue de Rennes and Boulevard Raspail the students were building a barricade of overturned cars, trash cans, and uprooted lamp posts. Behind me a caravan of police riot trucks was rolling toward the barricade. It stopped about a hundred yards from the students' street fort. The policemen outfitted in green fatigues, black helmets, goggles and paratrooper boots and fortified with billy clubs and shields filed from the trucks and formed a phalanx. The students armed with cobblestones charged the government's formidable line of defense. The authorities retaliated with blasts of tear gas and sorties of free-swinging riot police.

I was in no man's land. The concierge of my apartment building sensed the impending battle and bolted the doors. The neighbors on the floors above were watching the spectacle from their balconies. As I dodged hurtling rocks and enraged policemen, I called and waved to one of my neighbors. Fortunately, he recognized me and within seconds opened the door. For the remainder of the evening I was a spectator of the rebellion below.

As I watched the street battle, I recalled the theme of the students' speeches at the Odeon Theatre the night before. Speaker after speaker emphasized the importance of self-discipline and self-government. The days of dependence were over for them. They were going to do what they wanted to do. I asked myself, "Do they know *what* they want? What will they achieve by this violence?"

Ten years have elapsed since the student revolution of 1968. The grandiose reforms proposed in those hectic days did not take root. However, the history of that event taught us that blind rebellion is not the road to independence.

Rebelling against dependence

The challenge to rebel against your dependencies is to do what you think is truly important to you. However, to change your ways without any vision of what you want is simply to rebel for the sake of rejecting dependencies. Behaving in this manner brings you a step closer to mental, emotional, and sometimes physical self-destruction.

When you headline the idea of rebellion in your mind, you picture yourself cutting the strings of dependence. In short, you tell this world to go to hell. As you grow older you rebel in your quiet way against the values forced on you in your youth. You label this rejection of the past a reassessment of values, but in fact you blame yourself for having been so idealistic and gullible. The more you experiment with new behaviors and ideas, the more you question the conventional wisdom of your elders, your church, and your government. You never externally rebel against these authorities, but you internally dismiss them and their values. In the end you see yourself internally adrift from your roles and your expected behaviors, but externally you discharge duties required of you. Living becomes a chore of getting things out of the way. You rationalize this split behavior between mind and body by telling yourself it is childish to act out your internal rebellion.

You use your rational modes of thinking to contain the fires of rebellion raging within you. You tell yourself that if you think and behave independently you will lose the order and control present in your family, in your work, and in your interpersonal relationships. There is too much security to lose and so much discomfort to encounter if you act out your rebellion against the irrational people, ideas, and systems which control you. You see yourself as the silent martyr suffering the injustices of this world. Martyrs usually died because their vision of reality was broader than that of their persecutors, whereas you die psychologically because you have neither vision nor courage. Your internal suffering caused by rebellious upheavals changes to the persistent pain of cynicism. Then your cynicism drifts into the flaccid states of skepticism and indifference.

These negative views of yourself result from a lack of vision rather than a desire to rebel. Although rebellion for its own sake does not make sense, nevertheless it does indicate to you that your tendencies to be free and personally creative are being stifled. Rebellion is the pain signaling you that you are psychologically unhealthy. It is time to find out what is important to you.

Not only do you view yourself negatively, but your state of rebellion affects the attitudes which you harbor toward people around you. You see their behaviors as so many threats to your well-being. You judge their kind words as deceptions to weaken your guard. Their friendly gestures are attempts to win you over to their way of thinking. Your watchword is: "Don't trust anyone." Altruistic behavior is the con game of controlling people. You come to believe that there is no inherent value to human nature. Only the power to control and to possess is valuable. Therefore, you and others are justified in using any means to gain power over people.

Finally, through your rebellion, you become what you despised, the master over other people. Yet, even to be a master you depend on having servants. In acting out of rebellion you become domineering or cynical, but in either case you have not effectively solved the problem of escaping dependency.

Because the power to control others is the objective of your rebellion, you act aggressively in your relationships with others. The goal of your communication is to get the upper hand. For example, as a husband or a wife you are circumspect but forceful in your demands. At no cost do you want your behavior to be shaped by the rewards of tenderness and affection. So you will initiate activities to create an environment in which your partner will be dependent on you. As the breadwinner the husband controls the purse strings which is the center of all other household activities. In gaining economic control over the partner in the early stages of the relationship the husband gradually increases his psychological dominance over the wife by using money as a reward or punishment. The aggressive behavior on the part of the husband in money matters is staged as his fiscal responsibility, but in fact his behavior is a furtive maneuver to control his wife's behavior. He is playing on her feelings of guilt and her desire for approval.

The wife also can control the husband's behavior by acting aggressively even though she functions in the role of homemaker. In due time they come to know one another's weaknesses. Rather than succumb to economic dependence and all its implications, the wife manipulates the husband into a dependent role by defying the husband's household budget. She will spend, and spend, and spend. He will become furious because he has lost control. His fury is really the result of being dependent on his wife's desire for approval. However, instead of approval she wants power and independence. Ultimately, he will yield to her demands without surrendering his ostensible dominance in the relationship, whereas she will yield to his pretended dominance without really becoming dependent on his money. The relationship is then characterized as a power struggle in which both seek to escape the control of the other.

The same dynamics of rebellion function in an employee-employer relationship. The employer who is obsessed with the idea of control will behave aggressively toward his employees to keep them aware of their dependence on him. His threatening behavior is calculated to raise the anxiety level of his employees. Because he fears losing his job, the anxious employee will be extremely docile. If employees in a group share similar anxieties, they band together out of a desire for survival. They plan to ward off the aggressor. When management and labor rebel against one another, they are rejecting their mutual dependence. Although both groups attempt to arbitrate their differences, in the final analysis force decides the important issues. Without vision arbitration is the use of reason to balance the irrational tendencies of opposing people. At best, we will achieve only minimum standards of behavior in the employer-employee relationship model characterized by dependence and rebellion.

If your rebellious thoughts are acted out, you tend to behave erratically. Because you feel threatened, you perceive danger lurking for you almost everywhere. Without evidence of any serious provocation, you verbally strike out against people. You can attribute your behavior more to your feelings than your objective assessment of the situation. Your inconsistent behaviors add to your feelings of confusion. You seek relief from the pain of confusion by becoming more dependent on someone, something, or some idea. But as you become more dependent you are more apt to rebel. You are caught in a vicious circle which can only be broken by using your rational tendencies to develop vision and freedom.

If you are controlled by other people your well-being is dependent on their behaviors. When they behave negatively toward you, they in effect attack you psychologically. You in turn react violently either in word or in action. You protest that they should not act that way toward you. Fundamentally, you are rebelling against their control over you. Instead of breaking this dependency you accept their control and rebel only when they use it negatively. This type of anger occurs when you depend on approval. You accept someone's control over you as long as you receive praise from them, but you become angry when you are criticized. The rage that you feel within you explodes in statements such as "You should not do that to me" or "You have no right to behave that way toward me." These verbalizations of anger clearly show that you expect other people to act correctly. Correctly means that their behaviors will conform to your ideas about the way the world should be. When people do not behave according to your expectations, you believe that something terrible will happen to you or that you will lose something.

You may think that anger is an expression of your independence, idealism, or self-respect. It is actually an act of rebellion against dependence. You become angry when you lose control of others, yourself, or events. You believe that your independence is dependent on controlling others. Your anger then is a result of two types of dependencies. You become angry in the complaining sense because you allow your well-being to depend on the actions of others, and you become angry in the rebellious sense when you recognize that being dependent in any manner is threatening your freedom to choose what you want.

Because your trust at one time or another was betrayed you become hostile. If you cannot depend on anyone, then everyone is a potential enemy. For example, after having been rejected in love, you bear a grudge toward all men and women. Your erstwhile source of contentment has now become the sour taste in your life. At one time you trusted your parents, your church, your country, your boyfriend, your girlfriend, and your friend, but your trust was violated. You are ready to rebel against all of them. However, you fail to realize that your hostility is the result of your irrational dependence on these people and institutions in the first place. Your feelings of hostility will persist until you stop being dependent on trusting others.

Overgeneralizing

Critical thinking about your life situation reveals to you how dependent you are on other people for approval, success, and comfort. If you are ignored or criticized, you become depressed. When you analyze your negative feelings, you discover that dependence will bring you happiness only when the world and the people in it are perfect. Upon further analysis you realize how silly it is to depend on others for your own well-being when they, like you, experience irrational tendencies. Having seen the deficiencies of human beings and having been duped by your former docility, you now rebel against all positive ideas.

When you are rebellious you generalize your negative experiences to the whole of reality. Formerly you totally accepted people, dogmas, ideologies, and institutions; now you totally reject them. Overgeneralization causes loss of perspective and discriminative thinking. The rebellious person has no positive reference point from which he can judge the importance of different behaviors and events. Nor can he discriminate the value of one person's behavior from another, because he assumes that all human behavior is negatively motivated.

The mistake of overgeneralizing the results of your analysis of the human situation underlies the negative attitudes, behaviors, and feelings that you suffer. Your state of rebellion is caused and maintained by this inaccurate thinking. From a few negative experiences you make a law extending to all of humanity, and then you conclude that all men act negatively because that is the law of humanity.

Your "I don't give a damn about anyone" attitude is the result of either/or thinking. Either the world must be all good or all bad. People are either trustworthy or not trustworthy. Since you have had enough negative experiences to convince you that the world is not all good, you conclude it must be all bad, or at least more bad than good. You conclude that there is no point in constructing a worthwhile life.

You can get rid of this pessimism by paying attention to your rational self telling you that a worthwhile life is built in steps. Your vision of a full life can become a reality if you choose to do what is important to you. Making the life that you want is the work of your freedom. If you do not think about what is important to you and if you do not liven up your days by choosing to do what you want, you will become dependent on a system of dull routines.

The Art of Listening to Yourself

Dialogue 7—Resolving annoyances constructively

Whenever you feel your blood coming to a boil, take a deep breath and turn on your creative imagination. If you let your violence run away with you, you will surely crack up either physically and/or psychologically. Probably fifty percent of our broken dishes, doors, windows, ashtrays, bones and bruised knuckles are caused by unchecked anger.

1. Think of all the people and types of people who "make you angry."

2. Think of all the situations which "make you angry."

3. What are major reasons why people and situations "make you angry"?

4. Ask yourself the following questions:

   Has my anger permanently corrected other people's behaviors?

   If I acted according to my values instead of my irrational dependencies, would I stand a better chance to solve the interpersonal problems that annoy me?

8. Does the System Pay Off?

Usually when you think of system, you visualize yourself performing activities in steps. For example, if you are going to study for an examination, you will put the subject matter in a certain order before you begin to review each section. As you study you will link one section to the next. When you have learned each step, you return to the beginning to put everything together in one system. Each time you rehearse all the steps together, your learning is more systematized. When you are tested, you externally perform the internal routine which you have mastered.

In your job you are using the concept of system everyday. You are usually trying to put your work in a definite order, provided no one has already done it for you. First you classify the Items. Then you place the classifications in some temporal or spatial order. For example, you will separate accounts receivable from accounts payable, and you will spend a certain amount of time working on each. Or maybe your work consists only in putting items in categories so that someone else may link the groups in an appropriate order.

Once the system is developed, then you pass people, events, and paper through it. Soon your responsibility is merely to monitor and feed the system.

Systematizing your life

To systematize your life is to arrange your ideas, values and behaviors according to what is most important to you. Most systems of living can give you a feeling of security. When you are guided by a system, you put your ideas, behaviors and feelings in a sequence. For example, you may have a set way of conducting yourself in social situations (a business luncheon, a cocktail party, a date, etc.). You have a clear idea of what you want and what you want to avoid. The ideas running through your mind are determined by your goals. When you meet people in a social situation, you use your ideas to help you choose the most effective behaviors to get what you want. The following diagram illustrates this system:

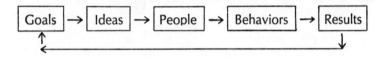

When you leave the social situation you feel either content or put out with yourself. If all went well, you will use the same system again. If you were unhappy with the results, you will adjust your system by changing one or all the components in the system. You might avoid certain types of people. Maybe you might meet the same people again, but you will change your ideas and behaviors. You will tinker with the system until you get what you want. The repetition of the sequence develops habits which are the actions representing what is important to you. Repeatedly behaving according to a logically coherent system of ideas increases your efficiency because you do not feel compelled to think through each new situation.

Your tendency to systematize your life can work for you or against you. If your system of life is rigid, it will prevent your emotional and mental development. By reducing your whole life to an unchanging system you become totally dependent on it. You surrender your power of critical thinking to the Frankenstein system which you created. On the other hand, when you pay attention to your tendencies pulling you to explore the unknown corners of your life, then your system is guided by your critical thinking.

In Chapter Thirteen you will see how the tendency to system-atize your life contributes to self-profit. However, systems can also work against you. The rest of this chapter is an exercise in using your best thinking to examine a rigid system controlling your ideas, feelings, and behaviors.

Trapped

How often do you feel confused because you want to do something different to enrich your life? Your system of ideas about life prevents you from doing something new. You want to return to school, but you will disrupt the family routine. You want to go on a vacation alone, but what will your spouse, children, neighbor, and relatives think about it. You have serious questions about your religion, but you had better not question too much or else you will lose your religion. Then you will have nothing to rely on. Instead of riding the current of life coursing through your mind, you prefer to freeze life into a system of manageable units. You feel miserable with yourself, but at least you have the joyless security which comes from obeying your system.

When the idea of system dominates your life, you see yourself as a self-made organization of finely crafted parts. You are simulta-neously the watch and the watchmaker. You design your words, your feelings, your ideas, your appearances, your desires, your skills, your relationships, and your goals so that they will mesh with one another. The synchronization of your vital activities is the key to a smooth life. Occasionally you clean the system when it is clogged with foreign matter. You discard all the new ideas, exciting feelings, and challenging actions which jar the balance of your delicately tuned life. If you allowed yourself to indulge in these novelties, you would run the risk of becoming a syncopated clock. But this would be catastrophic, because the watchmaker would lose control of the watch's rhythm. It is better to encase your ideas, feelings, and actions in the protective hardware of a system.

As long as you assume to know the limitations of your ideas, feelings, and actions, then you believe that you can accurately predict your future performances. Having this knowledge of your-self, you set goals within your limitations. Obviously you will achieve a high percentage of your goals. The purpose of a system is to yield higher productivity. In the case of your human behavior, the output is the satisfaction you feel in the accomplishment of a goal. You also desire satisfaction as you proceed through each step leading to the goal. You do not want to be frustrated or to waste time on matters deterring you from your goal. You feel valuable when you are efficient.

As long as you succeed you will have positive attitudes toward yourself. To maintain a positive attitude you must be careful not to miscalculate your abilities or to inflate your goals. At all times you must have your feelings under control, your ideas well ordered, and your actions carefully thought out. If you do not maintain stability within each component of the system, your reputation for efficiency and achievement will be seriously jeopardized. Failure is unbearable because you have identified yourself with your system. Thus, when the system fails, you are a failure. Your self-worth is scrapped with the system.

Marriage or any relationship can be systematized. For example, the components of the marriage relationship are wife, husband, father, mother, homemaker, wage earner, lover, and communicator. Then you have ideas about the required behaviors for each component. All other ideas and feelings that you have about your personal goals, such as a career, form a sub-system to the primary system of marriage. When both partners subscribe to the system, they experience a measure of satisfaction which is derived from accomplishing the prescribed behavior of each component. There is no room in the system for conflict. Consequently, conflict is avoided. You submerge any strong feelings or ideas about your own meaning of life because you are afraid to disrupt the system. You trade your internal dynamic security for the satisfaction of external security. Soon you realize that you have become dependent on the institution or habit of marriage. You lost everything the system was supposed to give you—happiness, security, and feelings of well-being and self-worth.

Trapping others

Not only is your attitude toward yourself conditioned by what is expected of you in your system, but also your view of others is determined by how well they conform to your expectations. People are good provided they are useful for your purposes. If you assess the thinking of your "friends," you will discover that they also are looking for the perfect system of living. You appreciate one another's company because you think alike. But as soon as one threatens the system of the other, the interest in each other dies. Your friendship was a pact of mutual usefulness. Plainly put, you had a business relationship in which the commodity was emotional satisfaction. In friendship as in marriage when you are guided by a rigid system you allow no room for conflict.

Because compatibility of systems is the basis for loving someone, love to you means useful behavior. Your enjoyment of another person and the other person's enjoyment of you depends on the mutual comfort you derive from each other's behavior. You are satisfied because the other person's behavior meets your expectations which is tantamount to saying that the other person fits into your system. You label the state of mutual satisfaction "love."

When the idea of system shapes your view of life, you begin to visualize people, events, and ideas as components of a grand system. You feel compelled to develop a program which will include everybody. The more comprehensive the system is, the better you feel. However, being a realist, you know that everyone does not fit your system. Consequently, you will attach yourself only to those people and ideas who fit in with your view of the world.

To change or not to change

You construct a system of living to behave regularly. Your daily responses are predictable because you have mapped out the behavioral patterns leading you to your goals. By reflecting each day on your major goals, such as advancement in your career, achieving an educational degree or a professional license, opening your own business, or improving the home atmosphere, you automatically think of the steps that you must take to realize these goals. Your system will work, that is, you will achieve your objectives provided you behave according to your program. On any given day you will be able to predict how you will behave, because you will not allow yourself to be drawn into situations which are beyond your control.

There is little room in your rigid system for spontaneity. You tend to treat surprises as temptations. You think that flirting too long with spontaneous feelings or events will shatter you. What is even more ominous, you believe that in being spontaneous you will not achieve your goal. Although spontaneous feelings, people and events at times almost overwhelm you, they never quite run away with you. You manage to get hold of yourself by focusing your attention on such slogans as "Be real," "Be practical," "Be sensible," "Stop wasting time," or "Get down to business." Consistency and parsimony are the hallmarks of the systematized person. Spontaneity, if not controlled, is like a time bomb within the system. The explosion of novel ideas represents an enormous threat to your tidy world.

Your world is static. You have chosen people and events to match your system. The breadth of your world is dependent on the boundaries of your system. But no system will be broad enough to embrace the multiplicity of ideas and people in the world. Philosophies, religions, life styles, and personalities which are not compatible with your system of reality are rejected. The center of your world is your threatened self. Only in a limited world will you be able to satisfy yourself in the achievement of your goals.

You will not be *fully* satisfied in simply following a system and achieving a limited goal. If you limit the world to fit your system, and if you limit your goals to fit your system, then you can experience only a limited satisfaction. The spontaneous feeling of desiring more will pressure the internal limits of your system until finally the boundaries will burst. At this point you will be confused because you may be afraid to explore new ideas, behaviors, and feelings. You felt safe in your system. Is it better to mend the fences of your old system or to explore the unchartered regions of the world within you and the world outside you? You are pushed to expand your vision and your freedom, but you are also pulled to end your confusion by staying dependent on a dependable system.

Your system and your affiliations

You experience great pleasure in knowing that you belong to some organization. Your feelings of worth and identity are usually dependent on your association with these groups. Often the system of ideas and values guiding your life is shaped directly or indirectly by these affiliations. Consequently, when your system of living conforms in outline to the ideals of the company, the church, the club, and the professional association, you feel that you have found your place. In addition to having a feeling of belonging you also experience a sense of worth. This feeling of worth is confirmed by the rewards of promotion, citations, and compliments bestowed on you by the organization. You express your gratitude by deepening your loyalty to the organization.

Although your feelings are usually under control, you are susceptible to a passive and simmering anger whenever your ideals are challenged. Serious criticism of your system or your affiliations stirs aggressive rumblings in your viscera. Since your own worth is identified with the ideals underlying your system, any attack on them is an attack on you. Usually the foes are people outside your ideal world. They are the ones whose behaviors and ideas are incompatible with your philosophy of life. Unfortunately, some of these people are very close to you. At times they are your own children. Even so, you cannot bear having your world attacked, so you do all in your power to silence the critics. Your tactics will show good taste, but nevertheless your objective will be deadly. Unless people conform to your ways they will be ostracized. Casting people out of organizations, homes, churches, and clubs is a common occurrence. Sometimes the separation is blunt and sudden; other times it is furtive and lingering. In the end you achieve the same objective—to get rid of the trouble-maker.

At times you feel anger because you are the victim of alienation. Although you dutifully adhere to your system of behaviors and loyally support your organization, you often go unrewarded. No one makes you feel that you really belong, because no one offers you significant promotions or praise. You are kept at an arm's distance—on the fringe. You become disgruntled because the system is not working for you, that is, you are not achieving those satisfying goals. You find yourself in a bind. If you act out your anger, your behavior will be inconsistent with your system. But on the other hand, if you do not act out your righteous anger, you will continue to suffer alienation. Adhering loyally to the system keeps you in the bind. Chances are that you will let your anger gnaw internally at you. Until you give up your dependency on the system, you will continue to suffer anger and alienation.

System thinking is not good enough

Analyze the way you build a system of living. You will discover that system building is the work of mechanical thinking. You spread out the parts of life so that your mind can classify them and put them in a proper order. Items such as wife, husband, mother, and father are grouped under roles. Money, success and happiness are labeled goals. Activities include working, studying, and loving. Then you have locations such as the home, the job, and the church. After categorizing the parts of your life you arrange them into systems and sub-systems. For example, the broad system may be doctor-work-office-hospital-money-success. Other roles, goals and activities would form sub-systems complementing the major system. Every item will have its place and its function. Each item is valued inasmuch as it contributes to the achievement of your final goal, success. From this perspective a problem means that a part of the life system is out of order. A solution means correcting the malfunctioning part so that the entire system will return to its former efficient ways. For example, if the wife or the children of the family develop systems of living incompatible with the husband's, then the husband is compelled to correct their systems to fit his; otherwise he will experience too much friction. And furthermore, controversy only leads to confusion and loss of time. Therefore, it would be better if everyone fit into one system.

This type of thinking is mechanical because you assume that each vital thought, event, feeling and relationship is a static thing over which you have absolute control. You also assume that everyone wants your goals. Furthermore you believe, without evidence, that your plan of life is the best one for everyone.

When you think mechanically you think uniformly. You fail to catch the subtleties and nuances of people's words and actions. You also miss the intricacies and potentialities of your own mind. In short, when you reduce all life to a system, then you believe that the vital is mechanical. You naively believe that solving human problems is only a matter of adjusting your behavior to a proper system.

Your thinking also tends to be practical when you live according to a system. Practical means that you set goals which are in keeping with your personal resources. Your level of expectation will never exceed your proven abilities. Therefore, your future is shaped by your past performances. This calculated view of the future protects you from the pain of failure. But the fear of failure prevents you from tasting the joys of discovery. You prefer a measured and predictable existence rather than an open and spontaneous life.

Your over-reliance on system is motivated by your doubts about the goodness of human nature. Usually you do not trust other people or yourself. You believe that your system of living, filled with don't's, protects you against your own weaknesses as well as the aggressiveness of others. If you violate your rules, you feel that you are losing control of yourself. Unless you mind your ways, you fear being dragged into the whirlpool of confusion. When the idol of system is destroyed by novelty, creativity, curiosity, or just a plain mistake, you feel empty, defenseless, and adrift.

Developing a system of life and conducting your life according to it can be to your advantage, provided your critical thinking is monitoring it. When you do not feel free to change your ideas and your behaviors, then you know that you are being defeated by your system.

The Art of Listening to Yourself

Dialogue 8—Checking the domino effect in your life

When one of your *irrational dependencies* guides the behaviors and feelings in one activity of your life, how do you behave and feel in your other activities? For example: Irrational dependency—I must be completely successful in everything I do at work. When I do not feel successful, I feel depressed. Then, as a spouse, parent and friend, I show little or no interest in the people who are close to me. When your *values* guide your behaviors and feelings in one activity of your life, how do you behave and feel in your other activities?

9. Changes

Change is the most common experience of your life. However, in your imagination you see your life as a series of still shots representing your past. The different images that you have of yourself from one stage of life to another make it difficult to know who you are. When you were young, you had ideas about the person that you wanted to become. Now that you are older you wonder if you have fulfilled that ideal. If you think of yourself as a collection of images, you soon become confused. Because you have so many conflicting pictures of your personality, you cannot get a handle on yourself. At one moment you feel secure about who you are because you identify well with your career and family roles. When you wonder if you are more than your roles, you undermine your sense of stability. Thinking that your roles do not fully define you and that your present is more than a collection of your past experiences, you are forced to stop seeing yourself statically. It is time to throw out the personal photo album filled with psychological snapshots. You begin to realize that the essence of living is to change.

Perhaps urban man's desire to return to the vital nature of the earth speaks not only of his innate reverence for the power and beauty of nature but also of his innate attachment to things alive and changing. You feel more at home in the forest than in the factory.

You are awed by the roaring thunder of the waterfall, but you are jarred by the cavernous rumbling of the subway. You feel peaceful by the seashore but anxious in the office. You sense that you belong with nature.

If you follow your innate tendency to identify yourself with the flow of life in nature, you will soon catch the meaning of change. You will feel your identity in feeling the power of life coursing through your body. The answer to who you are is found in accepting and knowing the changes that you feel and in choosing to live by those deep-seated feelings.

Dissatisfaction with yourself is traced to empty expectations. In examining the way you formulate your future, you discover how naive you are about the dynamics of human change. For example, your romantic ideas about love and marriage amount to a series of "should be's"—that is, he or she should be intelligent, beautiful, understanding, and tolerant. Then, after you are married, you should live in a certain place, should have so many children, should be secure as you enter the twilight of life. Love, then, is the satisfying feeling that you experience in the fulfillment of your "should be" images. When the future, as you planned it, is not coming true, you abandon the possibility of love and you accommodate yourself to a bland routine sprinkled with moments of passing pleasures and evanescent joys. Your disappointment is rooted in your shallow ideas and experiences of life. You see life as a series of things that should be done instead of a series of internal and personal moments exploding into external novelty. You erroneously think of happiness as a time in the future when you can relax because you will have everything that you want. In truth you do not know the possibilities of the next moment, the next day, the next relationship, or the next job, but you do know that those possibilities are present within the depths of each personal moment of existence.

The more attentive you are to your powers of knowing and willing, the more you are aware of your power to respond creatively to changes in people around you. Love is an encounter with life, but life is not perfect. Therefore, love is not perfect. Yet you violate your good sense when you expect people to behave in a

irrational

way that you think that they should. Your common sense tells you that life is a process of creative novelty. It is only reasonable then to expect spontaneity and surprises from other people.

Ironically, you reject the only *should* that may add meaning to life, and that is death. You can say that you *should* die, because *all* people die. However, the reality of your death confuses you because it is *the* contradiction to life. You prefer not to think about it. But in viewing life against the background of death, you sharpen your interest in life. Because you may lose your life at any moment, you can no longer take it for granted. However, you can escape the feeling of anxiety about your death by thinking of yourself in mechanical terms. Machines stop. You can believe that the end of your existence is nothing more than a final stop. By thinking mechanically of your existence you may escape the anxiety of dying, but you miss the joys of living spontaneously and creatively. However, your common sense tells you that you are a living being and not a machine. Death forces you to ask yourself, "What am I living for now?" Enjoyment is the answer. You experience enjoyment in the exercise of your vital powers. When you know that you are knowing, when you feel that you are feeling, when you will that you are willing, then you feel good about living.

Every being of nature has a beginning and an end, except nature itself. From start to finish every moment of each being is rich with the actualities of the past and the possibilities for the future. Each moment of life is different from and incomparable to past or future moments. Human life is not a system of preordained stages through which you pass mechanically. Nevertheless, you do divide your life according to time segments and label them as the childhood years, the adolescent years, the young adult years, and the mature years. Accepting these labels as true descriptions of your life, you believe that certain attitudes, behaviors, thoughts, and feelings belong specifically to each stage. This type of thinking makes it inappropriate for senior citizens to be romantic, for young people to be wise, and for middle-age people to be spontaneous, trusting and enthusiastic. When the expectations of each stage have been mapped out for you by society and have been accepted by you, you contradict your most valuable intuitions about human life. Intuitively, you know that your life is more than the routine rites of passage from one stage to another. You know there are stages in life, but you also know that each stage is the living moment embracing all the memories of the past and unleashing the creative powers of the present to shape the future.

Creative persons see themselves as beings in process. Time for them is not measured from beginning to end, that is, from birth to death. Time for them is life now. Every moment of their existence is novel and spontaneous because they refuse to let themselves sink into routine. They assimilate what is around them, they ponder what is in them, and they give to those near them. Young persons do not worry about losing their youth. Old creative persons do not pine over having lost their youth. And creative middle-aged persons are neither depressed nor anxious about the past or the future. Why? Each moment of life is incomparable, and what is important to each moment—love, joy, freedom, and hope—is present in every other moment in a different and richer way. If you develop your intuition of life to deepen and broaden your vision of your human existence, you will feel that you are in charge of yourself. Life does not slip away from you. You throw it away by not thinking critically, by not behaving freely, and by not feeling spontaneously.

The feeling of power is a sign of being alive. Viewing yourself as a person in the process of growing imparts feelings of confidence in your capabilities. Although you have some knowledge of your potential, you do not know the boundaries of your creative capacities precisely because you are changing. You are quite ignorant of the human potential in general. Only in testing the frontiers of your intellectual, volitional, moral, and physical powers will you be more creative. True power then is not in having things but in being and doing. Power is a lasting and internal energy which comes from a true understanding of man's mental, emotional, and physical processes. All external powers, such as money, fame, and political acumen, are useful and lasting insofar as they are employed to advance the consciousness of man.

People who use external power such as money and political power to confuse people and to make them dependent will in the end become confused within themselves. How often does this occur in families where parents attempt to control their children through the use of money. True power does not aim to control. It intends to create. Powerful persons govern by attraction and not by constriction. Their actions are invitations for others to do the same.

Accepting change in others

Invoking the golden rule of doing to others as you would have others do to you is very practical in developing a tolerant attitude toward other people who are continually experiencing changes in their lives. When you have accepted the idea that change is the essence of your experiences, you are ready to be empathetic toward the changing behaviors, attitudes, ideas, and feelings of the people closest to you. Just as you would appreciate an understanding of your own changing ideas about important matters from people near to you, so also it is only common sense that you attempt to understand their changing attitudes. However, you know that you are rarely tolerant of change in someone else. At those times when you are, you are usually biting your lip for fear of blurting out your true feelings.

You may ask why you expect others to accept changes in you while you do not expect others to change? Did you ever catch yourself saying, "I never expected him to do something like that." People are shocked by changes in people close to them because they consider something valuable to be unchanging. It is the old "true blue theory." In your mind the people you value are reliable and consistent, which means that they hardly change at all. When they change their behaviors, ideas and feelings, your respect for them is put to the test. You ask yourself, "Do I love and respect him unconditionally or do I love him because his ideas, feelings and behaviors are acceptable to me?" If your relationships to loved ones are based on unchanging ideas about those persons, then you are headed for disappointment, frustration, and confusion. Have you ever expressed your intolerant attitudes in statements such as the following:

"When we got married you were so different."

"You used to be a nice kid."

"Remember the good old days?"

"Ever since he has been going around with her, he has changed."

Adopting an accepting attitude toward the inevitable changes in other people creates a mentally healthy view toward people close to you. You will soon learn that your love for them is your concern for their well-being. Your respect for their freedom to choose what they believe will make their life meaningful. Unfortunately, not everyone chooses wisely. Although people are always changing, it is obvious that these changes are not always for the good of the individual. Sometimes your love for someone whom you think has gone astray drives you to the point of wanting to get inside him to straighten him out. Your unsolicited and persistent advice is usually interpreted as nagging. You will truly be more helpful to people close to you when you accept in others what you experience in yourself, namely, that life is change.

At times it is difficult to know whether your experiences of the moment are positive or negative. Your actions are meaningful when you judge them within the perspective of your whole life. Some events you can confidently label as valuable or worthless, but there are those that leave you in doubt. If you can live with this uncertainty, then it is only reasonable to assume that others will experience a measure of uncertainty in their human development. What binds people together is not an agreement on unchanging ideas but a respect for each other's quest for truth and meaning.

The Art of Listening to Yourself

Dialogue 9—Directing the changes in your life

1. What behavioral changes do you want to make in each activity of your life?
   Examples:
   — from acting indecisively to acting decisively
   —from behaving shy to behaving confident
   — from lounging around to exercising physically
   — from smoking to not smoking
   — from not listening to listening

2. What mental changes do you want to make?
   Examples:
   — from overgeneralizing to being specific
   — from quick to judge to taking my time

— from talking before thinking to thinking before talking
—from fantasizing to thinking about the value of my life
— from putting myself down to accepting myself
— from thinking pessimistically to thinking optimistically

3. What feelings do you want to change?
   Examples:
   — from anxiety to confidence
   — from mistrust to trust
   — from despair to hope
   — from depression to joy
   — from hate to love
   — from being left out to belonging
   — from frustration to achievement
   — from boredom to enthusiasm
   — from hostility to friendliness
   —from jealousy to magnanimity

Part Four

WHOM CAN YOU TRUST?

10. Having Doubts

Trust is an old-fashioned virtue. In the past the grocer, the butcher, and the baker could expect their customers to pay their bills. You could even rely on the train being on time. In big cities you could leave the front and back doors of your house open without worrying about being robbed. To get cross-ventilation during the hot and muggy summer months neighbors in apartments would leave their doors open almost all evening. Little kids could ride public transportation just for the fun of it. In most of our dealings with other people we could expect honest and decent behavior. If we have never personally experienced this simple trust in human nature, we have read about it or have heard older generations talk about it. The stories of the family doctor taking a personal interest in the children whom he visited are pictures of human nature that awaken in us a strong desire to trust our fellow human beings. Today, a sophisticated skepticism seems more in step with the pace of events. If we allow ourselves the psychological luxury of being trustful, we feel that we will soon be financially poor. After all we live in a competitive society where success is the criterion for most of our behavior. Trusting other people, so we are led to believe, can only encourage them to take advantage of us. But we do not want to insult others by communicating our mistrust to them. Instead we choose to be charmingly inquisitive about their concerns, while in reality we are sizing them up.

The desire to trust the better side of human nature clashes with many prevalent social attitudes about people's selfish tendencies. The negative view of people encountered daily in the newspaper, on TV, and in gossip reinforces our skeptical attitude toward the positive tendencies in our fellow human beings and in ourselves. Reviewing our unfulfilled expectations we tend to be pessimistic about the future. Yet the desire for a better life persists underneath all our negative attitudes. Because we are torn in two directions we feel uncomfortable. The more we experience the pull in opposite directions, namely, wanting to trust and behaving without trust, the more we experience the pain. We can immediately minimize this discomfort by choosing to follow one tendency or the other. If we opt for skepticism, then we relax the longing to be trustful. However, it remains to be seen which decision is more beneficial in the long run.

There was a time when we were hopeful and optimistic about the future. In our youth we had grand expectations about love, a career and marriage. Our ideal values were shaping up nicely into a blueprint for human happiness. Day by day we would try to construct realities from our romantic ideals. Then we began to run into snags because everyone, including ourselves, was not doing what he or she should to do. People at work were hindering us from advancing in our careers. We soon found out that all people cannot be trusted. In our interpersonal relations we discovered many dark corners within ourselves and within the person whom we thought we loved. Before long we became disillusioned with others and ourselves. We realized how naive and immature we were.

Often our disillusionment turned to a simmering rebellion. All those people and institutions who filled our heads with lofty notions about life deceived us. We soon rejected them and their ideals. But the pain of separating ourselves from our church or our parental values was almost as agonizing as suffering from disillusionment. As a result we have never completely rid ourselves of either pain.

Although we have toned down our expectations about ourselves and others and have doubted the goodness of life itself, nevertheless we secretly long for the fulfillment of a happy life. We limit our goals to cushion ourselves from the pain of disappointment. But we still work hard at achieving our modest objectives—in fact, probably harder than when we were harboring those grandiose goals for ourselves. By laboring more diligently to achieve less, we think that we protect ourselves from the pain of failure. Happiness for us has become an escape from physical and psychological discomfort. Our best bet, then, to insulate ourselves from the negative feelings in life is to disembowel ourselves of our visceral attachment to life. We believe that we can pass through life uninvolved and unscathed by freezing our ardent passion to live each day to its fullest.

It would seem logical to give up all hope for happiness if we followed fully our skeptical tendencies. But the pain of despair can be deadened only by exiling ourselves from society. When we despair, we gnaw at ourselves with images of what we might have been. Every day is filled with reminders of our dashed hopes. Our job is only a symbol of an unfulfilled career goal. The interpersonal conflicts and tepid relations with our spouse and children are sharply silhouetted against our youthful dreams of a happy home. If we despair of ever recouping our enthusiasm for life, then we let ourselves slip into anonymity through drink, drugs or some other physical escape. If, on the other hand, we choose to function in our job and our family, then we stop short of despair. Skepticism holds us on a steady course between giving up and engaging life. We see no reason to struggle for ideals which will never come true, nor do we see any sense in permitting ourselves to wither away. To fall into despair is an acknowledgement of a loss of a deep value, but to remain skeptical is to be noncommittal about any values. The skeptic is not ready to leap into the abyss of nothingness.

A veiled wish for a better life lingers under our "wait and see" attitude toward life. In spite of our pessimism, from time to time we experience positive feelings in our work and with the members of our family. Because we enjoy these moments, we feel a tendency to regain our erstwhile zest for life. But our "we know better" selves hold these frivolous moments in check. We warn ourselves not to be carried away by the joy of the moment. Past experience taught us that hoping for the best ultimately leaves us feeling the worst. In spite of protecting ourselves from our temporary positive feelings, a constant but low-keyed desire to trust ourselves and others persists. Because we are aware of the pluses in our lives, we feel the tension between hope and despair.

We protect ourselves from despair by limiting our hopes. We

think that by reducing life we can increase our trust in life. We practice these ideas by narrowing our range of concerns in the major areas of our life. Love for our family is reduced to providing or servicing the physical needs of our spouse and children. We have already reasoned that the word "love" has no meaning because people in general cannot be trusted. Without trust what can love mean?

Achieving a career becomes surviving at a job. The novelty of the challenge has faded, and routine has set in. Instead of working to create and advance ourselves we do our job to protect our job. Again, there is no one trustworthy out there.

Our circle of friends shrinks to a smaller circle of acquaintances. Each move toward desocialization is an attempt to achieve maximum trust in others by minimizing our involvement. Intellectually, we can clearly see the contradiction of skepticism, but emotionally we are blinded by our past hurt feelings. Rather than suffer rejection and deception at the hands of people close to us, we prefer to live the contradiction of skepticism.

The skeptic usually engages in a pattern of behavior which is predominantly passive. If you have little trust in the goodness of life, then you will be wary to extend yourself to others. How many times have you volunteered your services to some organization only to have someone neglect your good will or even to be rude to you. The lesson of keeping to oneself is quickly learned from those experiences. From now on, you tell yourself, you will say little and the little you say will mean little. These negative experiences with other people convince you of your early suspicions about the inherent selfishness of people. You reserve your spontaneous outbursts for light occasions like parties and ballgames. In serious matters it's best to play the part of the somewhat concerned but quiet bystander.

At times passivity can be an effective and subtle form of aggression. For example, by not responding to your spouse in an argument you show your doubt about his or her intentions. The arguing stops but the feeling of alienation intensifies. It would be better to continue arguing—not that a barrage of words flung at each other solves the problem, but at least there is a primitive type of communication. Silence invites you to think the worst thoughts about each other. In silence the pain of alienation is heightened to the point where the relationship is ready to crumble. But the pain of complete separation from someone whom you are supposed to love might be greater than the annoyances experienced in your regular misunderstandings. Because you doubt that divorce would give you a better life, you look for ways to break the silence. So what have you gained by withdrawing? Nothing. Instead of confronting your spouse's intentions and thereby putting your own suspicions to the test you prefer to presume that his or her words and actions are motivated by selfishness. Your last-minute rescue attempt barely holds the relationship together. Time after time the same scene occurs—disagreement, silence, and rescue. If two people had a trusting attitude toward each other the scene would be: disagreement, honest communication, and renewed trust.

Deception is another behavior trait of the skeptic. Perhaps there was a time when your survival in your job was at stake. When your back was against the wall, your real attitudes toward others played themselves out in your behavior. Rather than relying on your own internal strength or the honesty of other people, you chose to protect yourself through deception. In order to make yourself look good, you planted the seeds of discord in the minds of your colleagues or co-workers. Then the competencies and loyalties of other people were questioned by the supervisor. In an atmosphere of declining morale and rising anxiety, you could present yourself as the loyal and efficient worker. If you were the threatened boss, you could have used the same tactic of raising the anxiety levels of the employees. Then you could have entered the scene as the savior.

Another form of deception is approval-giving. People who are unsure of themselves need reassurance especially from authority figures or successful people. The skeptic appears as a warm and concerned person to dependent people because he tells them what they want to hear. The same people who complain about people in authority are the first ones to swoon at the boss's compliments. Their complaints are shouts for attention. The skeptic, well aware of this human weakness, dispenses his calculated approval for his own benefit. Perhaps you have experienced being on one end or the other of this situation. Eventually you probably realized the phoniness of the approval given and the weakness in yourself or vice versa. At that moment of awareness you could have chosen to put an end to your feeling of dependence and your deceptive behavior. If you stop being dependent, it makes the approval giver squirm in his deception. Likewise, if you stop showering approval, it forces the dependent person to approve himself.

The feeling of alienation is almost a constant condition of the skeptic. Ordinarily, alienation can be traced to a number of social causes such as prejudice and parental rejection. But even in those cases there are times when you feel identified with some people. The desires to feel wanted and loved overcome the tendency to distrust everyone. However, if you fight off the desire to be loved and to love, then you bring upon yourself a state of alienation. The choice to avoid a close and trusting relationship is a poor substitute for occasional rejections.

This constant feeling of not belonging to anyone is the logical conclusion of the major beliefs of skepticism. Once you have established the premise that no one is trustworthy, then the conclusion of remaining aloof follows logically. When you believe that close relationships inevitably end in disastrous results for yourself, you will avoid trusting anyone. And without trust in someone you will be without friends. Without trust in yourself no one will be attracted to place trust in you. So the feeling of not belonging to anyone is caused by not believing in anyone.

Apathy follows right on the heels of alienation. When you cut yourself off from people, you sever yourself from the flow of life. All your powers of vision, freedom, and creativity require people for their realization. Intellectual and emotional growth occurs only by intra- and interpersonal communication. But unless you believe that happiness is the use of your human powers, growth is impossible. The process of being happy cannot begin without risking yourself to trust someone. Because the skeptic is unwilling to take the chance of trusting anyone, he never tastes the fullness of life. He expects little from life; therefore he invests himself sparingly in anything that he must do. Consequently, his feelings are uniform. There is no high or low—just a constant drone to his existence. Even the most striking accomplishments of man, such as the Venus de Milo and Mona Lisa, leave him emotionally flat. His own actions are performed routinely. Day after day he performs the same sequence of

events without any emotion so that eventually the days are indistin-
guishable.

When you feel burdened with apathy, check your attitude of
trust and your hope for a fulfilled life. Whining and dragging yourself
around are clues that you are giving in to skepticism. It is time to
turn your attention to the values and goals in life which are most
important to you. It is also time to focus on your freedom, that is,
your power to choose the person you want to be. To yield to
discouragement and disappointment is equal to saying that other
people control your life, and so far they have not been controlling it
for your benefit. So you tear yourself from this misery by withdrawing from people. This strategy is ineffective because in a roundabout
way other people are still really controlling you. Your withdrawal is
a reaction to them. You are in control when you see what you want
and choose it, and not when you see what you don't want and
spend all your time avoiding it.

Unless you challenge your skeptical tendencies, you will rapidly feel depressed. Depression is a feeling which results from
negative judgments about yourself. After distrusting human nature in
general and scoffing at the idea that humans will improve themselves, you can easily convince yourself that life is absurd. There is
no hope for people and no hope for you. There are no goals
and no values. Any glimmer of hope flickering in the hollow depths
of your skepticism is extinguished by your judgment about your
own worthlessness. Why survive? There is no reason.

The feeling of depression is the logical conclusion of the assumptions of skepticism. In the final analysis you will become what
you believe. But the skeptic believes that man is irreparably distorted. Soon he believes that he himself is also valueless. In spite of
his previous boasting about his objective and realistic attitude toward life, he suffers depression because of his own subjective and
distorted attitudes about people. When you begin to feel blue, catch
yourself quickly before falling into the quicksand of skepticism. You
need a basic trust in yourself and other people in order to build a
solid foundation for your emotional, intellectual, and social growth.
Without trust, the more you struggle to get out of your problems,
the more you sink into depression.

A strict analytical thought process based on the assumption

that you can't trust anybody functions almost impeccably in the mind of the skeptic. He is forever sizing up situations and people. Until he can label every intention behind each behavior he will be internally restless. Because of his long practice at figuring out people's motives, he fancies himself as a shrewd observer of human nature. So he will pick apart people until he feels sure that he has discovered the real reasons for their actions.

Paradoxically, the skeptic trusts the power of analytic thinking to give him certainty about people's motives. The obsessive desire for certainty makes the skeptic. In trusting people you do not have absolute certitude about their behavior toward you, because their motives are not apparent. In fact, sometimes the people themselves are unaware of what is pushing or pulling them to act in a given way. Yet, the skeptic wants to be able to predict people's behavior. By not trusting people he eliminates the element of surprise because he expects people to behave out of selfishness. He simply refuses to be impressed if people appear to act altruistically. Experience has convinced him that in the end the consequences of these actions satisfy the selfish desires of the do-gooder.

The skeptic supports his line of reasoning about human nature by appealing to history, psychology, and sociology. He can cite example upon example depicting the distortions of human nature. However, the skeptic fails to see that these distortions are not the essence of life. He refuses to push his mind to see the realities which are beyond appearances. If you accept a positive side to human nature in addition to a negative side, the task of understanding and predicting human nature becomes complicated. You are forced to function in many gray areas of human behavior. But as I said before, the paradox of the skeptic is his desire for certainty. He cannot live in gray areas. Consequently he reduces all human behavior to one dimension, the negative behaviors of people.

You have probably used either/or thinking. Examples are: love me or leave me; love your country or leave it; you are either with me or against me; I am either good or bad. This type of thinking can lead you to illogical conclusions because you tend to interpret one negative action on someone's part as being representative of his total attitude toward you. It's the typical mistake of generalizing your opinion about someone from a small piece of his behavior.

The skeptic favors the negative side of man. If you practice this either/or thinking and your conclusions about yourself and other people are usually negative, you might be imperceptibly developing a skeptical attitude. It is easy to let your thinking slide into these lazy and sloppy ways of judging reality. Life is too varied. It does not permit itself to be labeled so simply. If you do not try to see all the lines and shades of life, you will miss the beauty of life. And what is worse, you will suffer all the negative feelings of pessimism. Little by little you will condition yourself to give all your attention to all that is worst in man.

One-dimensional or surface thinking gives you a distorted view of the world. It is like being held prisoner in the hall of mirrors at the amusement park. Every reflection of a human being is grotesque. Your ways of thinking about yourself and others are the mirrors. To dispel this continual nightmare, change your ways of thinking; otherwise you are on the way to self-destruction.

The Art of Listening to Yourself

Dialogue 10—How to spot your skeptical self and how to develop trust in yourself

1. Make a list of the people you do not trust.

2. Next to each person give your reason why you do not trust him or her.

3. Next to each person identify the situation in which you do not trust him or her—for example, in a business relationship, in a personal relationship, etc.

4. Next to each person describe how you feel in his or her company—for example, defensive, inferior, anxious, etc.

5. Check to see:
   (a) if you distrust different people for the same reason;

(b) if you distrust people in certain relationships with you (for example, you might tend to distrust people more in a business relationship than in a social relationship);

(c) if you experience the same feeling with these different people.

6. Check to see if you follow a pattern in not trusting people. For example, you might have a skeptical attitude more in business situations with people who are aggressive. You might generally feel defensive and inferior in their company.

7. Ask yourself if your skepticism is the result of someone else's behavior or of your lack of confidence in your own abilities. If you feel defensive and inferior in the company of others, you probably do not think much of yourself. When you think little of yourself, you feel powerless.

8. Make a list of all your positive qualities. Then list five things which are most important to you. Put one of your positive qualities to work by doing one thing which is important to you. For example, if independence is important to you and one of your positive qualities is being even-tempered, then initiate a conversation with a person you distrust about a topic with which you usually feel uncomfortable. For example, you might not trust someone at work because he or she is always trying to put you down or get something on you. You will feel a sense of power. You will also learn to trust your own judgments.

If you repeat this exercise with different people in different situations, you will discover that you control other people's negative behaviors best by initiating your own positive behaviors.

11. How Certain Do You Have to Be?

Some years ago I was teaching a high school class. In the next classroom there was a chemistry teacher who managed his class so efficiently that he could boast of not wasting a minute. His classes were meticulously planned to the point that he would use a stop watch to time his quizzes. His instructions for classroom procedures were given by snapping his fingers. One snap meant pens down. Two snaps meant pass your papers forward. One snap and two quick snaps meant something else. And so on. The students performed with more precision than the Swiss watch which he used to time them. That classroom was a world where people behaved on cue. As soon as "Fingers"—that's what the kids called him—left the classroom, all hell broke loose.

Then the language teacher followed the chemistry teacher. He would always pace off the same number of steps to his desk, place his briefcase on the upper left corner of the desk, walk to the window to adjust it slightly, march back to the desk, and take out his books. After this ritual he would begin to teach the unruly mob in front of him. Oblivious to the students' antics he would scrupulously perform his lesson plan, pack his books, bid good afternoon, and leave for his next class.

I often wondered how Fingers and Robot Man—that's what the kids called the language teacher—functioned outside the classroom.

But if you think about their behaviors there is a bit of fingers and robot man in all of us. We want other people to behave predictably. Rather than snapping our fingers we use subtle ways of controlling someone else's behavior. At times we withdraw or play hard to get in order to attract attention. When we disapprove, we frown or show our displeasure by keeping an icy silence. We are really trying to get everyone in the place where we want them. The benefit of having everyone behave according to our own standards and expectations is security. We feel sure of ourselves when our social environment is predictable. As long as our spouse, children, friends, employers, and employees do what they are supposed to do, all will be well with us. Given that assumption, we feel that we must commit ourselves to shape people's behavior according to our designs. Our mental comfort depends on how much everyone agrees with us. When our children choose the careers and colleges that we planned for them, we sport a smile of self-satisfaction. If they waste their education in frivolous distractions, we boil with anger. We are upset because we believe that our children will amount to nothing if they do not adhere to our plans. When our blueprint for their happiness is not followed, then their future careers and our future states of mind, so we believe, will be insecure. We react angrily to their unruly behavior because we have made our own happiness depend on their achievement. The more radical problem is our own inability to live with insecurity. It is natural to think of a definite plan of action to change one of our unsettled situations. However, it is irrational to assume that we have absolute control over other people's behavior.

At times you may be gripped with an obsessive desire to be a hundred percent sure before you do anything. You may experience this feeling at work. You go over a problem numerous times so that you will feel absolutely sure about your course of action. After several analyses you no longer come up with new ideas. In the rest of the time that you spend thinking, you are no longer reacting to the problem but to your fear of making a mistake. Instead of acting immediately on your best knowledge you train yourself in that extra time to behave anxiously. You have taken a perfectly rational procedure—analysis—and through your excessive desire for certainty turned it into an irrational nightmare—scrupulosity. If you look at these behaviors closely, you will see that what you are really after is someone's approval. You are afraid to make an error because your boss or your colleague will criticize you for it. You can put up with making mistakes as long as no one finds out.

If you are in the habit of equating your personal value with perfect behavior, then making mistakes has dire psychological consequences for you even in private. You probably destroy anything you do which is not perfect. Whether you act for approval or absolute perfection, you can see that the rational tendency for certainty can be used to encourage your irrational dependencies. In the first case you perform ineffectively because you depend on someone's approval, and in the second case your self-worth depends on being perfect. The problem, then, is to learn how to use the rational tendency for certainty in a way which will help you behave freely and creatively.

There are some questions you can ask yourself which will help to clarify the apparent conflict that exists between the desire for certainty and the uncertainty of desire.

Do I desire to be spontaneous?

Do I desire to do new things?

Do I desire to be exciting?

Do I desire to grow?

Do I desire to change?

If you answered *yes* to the above, then you are in touch with your more than rational tendencies. Now ask yourself the following questions:

Do I expect to perform predictably always?

Do I expect to feel the same always?

Do I expect other people to accept my behaviors always?

Do I expect my feeling of well-being to depend on someone else's feelings about me?

Do I expect absolute certainty in everything I do?

If you answered *yes* to all the questions in the second group, it is clear that your tendency for certainty leads you to think that you are better off when you are unchanging. That is, you want your goals, your actions, your feelings, and your ideas to stay the same. But if you answered yes to all the questions in the first group you probably experience the contradiction of simultaneously wanting to change and not to change. You are afraid to change, because you fear the unknown. You are also afraid because you are not sure what you might find out about yourself. This is the contradiction. You try to be certain about everything around you so that you will be protected from the uncertainty about yourself. As long as everything around you is in its place, you will not be challenged to test your personal strength. The certitude that you think you have is really ignorance. You convince yourself out of fear that you are more sure of yourself by avoiding the feelings of uncertainty raised by your tendency to act freely.

·If you want to know if you are the type who prefers to be predictable rather than spontaneous, ask yourself the following questions:

Do I always tell myself the type of person that I am? For example: I am retiring, I am unsure of myself in social situations, I am dull and boring.

Do I always foresee and exaggerate the possible pitfalls in everything that I am about to do?

Do I usually shuttle my mind between reasons for doing something and reasons for avoiding the same thing?

Do I prefer to behave according to a daily routine rather than to try new activities each day? For example: Go to a different restaurant at lunch, take a different route to work, read a different newspaper.

Do I rigidly apply a set of ideas to direct my behaviors with other people?

Do I feel uncomfortable when I act contrary to the image I have of myself?

Do I frequently get angry with myself?

If you answered yes to all these questions, then you probably consider yourself to be a predictable person. When you act according to a plan, you feel a sense of achievement and self-satisfaction. The most important self-reward is your judgment about yourself which says that you are mentally and emotionally fine if you perform well externally. When you have achieved your goals on a few occasions, you expect to realize all your plans in the future. After each success you define yourself in terms of what you did. For example, "I am a good salesperson, tennis player, executive, teacher, artist, or writer." You also define yourself in terms of how you did it. "I am aggressive, patient, pragmatic, unemotional or persistent." Then in the future you expect to experience the same outcomes from the same behaviors. You feel secure about the future because your feelings and actions are under the control of the ideas you have about yourself.

The only way to maintain that safe feeling about yourself is to defend the ideas which guide your actions. For example, if you believe that you are a responsible person and that responsible means doing what is required of you, you will fulfill all your obligations to the letter. You will be the biggest breadwinner, the most meticulous housewife, the scrupulous student, or the conservative executive.

When you experience feelings about yourself contrary to the image you have of yourself, you ignore or bury these unwanted feelings under a barrage of self-statements which remind you of your self-image. If you are a responsible executive, you are supposed to act cautiously. There is no place in your self-image for strong feelings of spontaneity. If you are the meticulous housewife, there is no room in your china closet for a spotted glass. In fact, you are telling yourself that to feel good about yourself you must live up to the image you have of yourself. Then you are forced to say that the image of yourself is your model for self-fulfillment. Your meaning of life consists in maintaining this closed system.

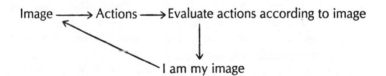

This system gives you a feeling of well-being provided you can eliminate or minimize your feelings of spontaneity, your desire for novelty and your feelings of surprise. These feelings threaten to destroy your image. Because you have identified yourself with your image, your emotional stability is threatened each time you desire to experience more joy and love of life.

Although you want to express your deep feelings of concern

toward people close to you or creatively communicate your inner responses to issues and situations, nevertheless you restrain these feelings welling up within you to the point where it physically hurts. But you would rather suffer the internal tension of holding back yourself, rather than risk being embarrassed. By holding a close rein on your feelings you believe that your thinking will be clearer and your percentage of error lower. You will not blurt out that expression of affection or that statement of discontent. In your mind you judge your behavior to be perfect because your image remains untarnished. Externally you feel successful, but internally you feel frustrated. All of your deep beliefs and feelings about yourself and others are smothered under your fear of public disapproval.

Believing that security and success are the rewards of certainty, you continue to fight against your tendencies to behave, think and feel spontaneously. You tell yourself that you will behave freely when you are more sure of yourself. Consequently, your desire to feel free is usually frustrated.

Ironically, when all your attention is focused on being certain about everything that you do, your performance is marked with hesitancy. You appear to be unsure about yourself. Reflect for a moment on those situations in which you were reminding yourself to do everything just right. You resemble the self-conscious bride mechanically approaching the altar. The congregation holds its breath as she precariously negotiates each step of the sanctuary. Or recall your first date, your first day at the office, your first honeymoon, your first public appearance, and so many other firsts. You were so concerned about doing everything right that you were unaware of what was immediately before you. Consequently your behavior was generally inappropriate.

I remember a salesman giving his first public address. His only concern was to get done with it without mispronouncing words. He rapidly moved along. His throat became parched. As he continued to speak, he reached for the pitcher of water on the table next to the podium. Then facing the audience without breaking his presentation, and unaware that there was no glass next to the pitcher, he simply poured the water on the table. The situation was both comical and embarrassing.

How many times have you experienced similar self-conscious

moments? If you analyze them, you have to laugh at yourself. When your mind is detached from the reality around you, you do funny and unexpected things. But if you do not check your obsessive desire to do everything perfectly, then you will feel frustrated. Perfection comes not by thinking about perfection but by thinking about what you are doing.

Whenever we are overly cautious about every thought and move that we make, we inevitably bring on ourselves the emotional and mental discomfort that we wanted to avoid. We behave scrupulously because we envision only disaster if the final outcome of our actions is not exactly as we planned. So we take great pains to control all the variables surrounding our course of action. Even though all our attention is concentrated on one act at a time, our overall performance is usually poor, and, at times, comical or tragic. In recent times we had the Watergate caper which exploded because a security guard noticed an open door that should have been locked. The most powerful government in the world began to crumble. We all know who and what was behind that door. The people who were so possessive about their political power took ridiculously extreme measures to annihilate every little threat. They wanted to be certain that what they had they would keep.

If you feel that you need to be absolutely certain about someone's affection, friendship, loyalty or honesty, you probably put him to the test by questioning his behavior. You want to know in detail all his thoughts and actions. After receiving the testimony of his undying love for you, you still harbor doubts about his real feelings. Not only are you skeptical about people's attitudes toward you, but you are also dubious about yourself. You endlessly question your abilities, your values, your goals, and your honesty. You engage in a type of questioning which is fruitless because you are prodded by skepticism, that is, a belief that you will never have absolutely certain answers to the questions about the purpose of human existence. Yet, believing that answers are never personally satisfying, you continue to raise the same questions over and over to yourself and others. This behavior annoys you and everyone around you. The belief in skepticism and the desire for certitude is a deadly combination. By holding on to both you will experience a mental strain that will express itself in scrupulous, complaining and blaming behaviors. You become so obnoxious to yourself and others that you reinforce your doubts about the goodness of yourself and others. You are caught in a vicious circle.

The way out of the certitude-skepticism whirlpool is learned by expecting novel instead of absolutely certain answers to your questions. A new point of view is mentally surprising; however, it may be practically threatening. If you translate a novel idea into a new behavior, you run the risk of experiencing the unexperienced consequences of that behavior even though you may cognitively know the outcome. But at times you perceive an enormous gap between *knowing* what will happen and *feeling* what will happen. You are excited by the new ideas, but not motivated enough to jump into action. When you are about to leap, you stop yourself with the realistic "but" arguments such as "I know he loves me, but to be sure I will . . ." or "I know I want to be a lawyer but. . . ." You convince yourself not to follow your new ideas and to be more realistic, that is, more skeptical, more pessimistic, more monotonous, and more ritualistic. Just as you are about to soar into novelty and to follow your best sense, you shut down your powers of intuition and perception. You tell yourself that your vision of reality is a dream, that your feeling of potential is an illusion, and that positive change is wishful thinking. "Be real. Keep your feet on the ground. You have everything to lose." In the end the warnings from the demon of skepticism keep you grounded. By listening to that self-talk prompted by fear you blur your vision of reality. The safe routine into which you lapse is a delusion of reality. Only by wanting and expecting newness, spontaneity, and creativity can you be real. By submerging or masking your deep and powerful feelings of being free and creative, you only sharpen the pain of alienation caused by not trusting yourself and others.

In a short time you can even manage to muzzle your outspoken curiosity. The prospect of thinking and behaving differently raises your anxiety level. You are comfortable with your routine even if you are not totally satisfied. When ideas about a new career, different values, or new friends enter your mind you focus immediately on the limitations within your reality instead of on the possibilities. For example, a housewife wanting to go to college or to enter business after twenty years in the home will think about her lack of experience in academics and office skills rather than about her ability and motivation to learn. The past becomes a criterion for today's action. Following this reasoning you are condemned to relive all your yesterdays. There is no future for you because there is no present. The advantage to this type of thinking is to be almost free from anxiety. For example, when you watch a movie for the second time you never feel the tension that builds as the characters and events unfold. In the first viewing you can foresee a variety of possible outcomes with each new revelation of a personality. Each is as plausible as the next. But in the second viewing you are mentally relaxed. Your curiosity extends only to the mechanics and technique of the film. Likewise in your life, you experience an excitement when you live in the present with a view to think and do something different. However, if you are immobilized by an excessive concern for certitude, then you prohibit yourself from even thinking about the possibility of being exhilarated.

Did you ever feel fatigued? Trace the events preceding this feeling. Go through your ideas and behaviors in slow motion. What outcome was motivating your mental activity? Maybe you felt fatigued during a party, after a date, during work, or just relaxing around the house. In each of these instances fatigue was not the feeling you wanted. But if you are washed out, you can suspect that your energies are being surreptitiously drained off by a pervading and camouflaged desire to be mistake-free. Appearing to have a good time at the party, you were more concerned about saying the right thing, keeping the conversation going, and making a good impression. You constantly felt yourself going against your authentic feelings, but you would not consciously admit the contradictions you were feeling. Preferring to keep up the front of self-assurance, you expended a volume of psychic and physical energy in holding down those visceral rumblings threatening your self-control. Likewise, at home or at work you feel fatigued because your mind is preoccupied with planning the next impeccable project. Every present moment is an opportunity to worry about the next moment. You even manage to justify your worrying behavior by appealing to your reason. It is perfectly reasonable to worry if your reason for living is to do everything perfectly. Fatigue, so you believe, is the price you pay for trying to achieve your goal. Now that everything fits logically, you are persuaded to continue your irrational behavior. However, there is one mistake which you made. You did not pay attention to your common sense, telling you through your deepest feelings that the purpose of living is to be free and not to be mistake-free. But the price of freedom is taking the risk of making a mistake.

Procrastination is another behavior caused by our excessive concern with being certain before we act. We usually impress upon ourselves the importance of our next step in getting the job that we really want, in marrying the person that we truly love, in buying the house that will completely satisfy us, or in expressing our arguments to the boss that will be sure to get us a promotion. We spend hours and days planning that next step. As we think about each possible action, we focus on the consequences of that action. Before long we begin to see only slight differences in the outcomes of several actions. But we want to know which action is absolutely bound to the consequences that we want. The debate within our mind begins and never ends. In the meantime the external world moves on. Someone else got the job that we wanted, our true love married someone else, and the house that we were thinking of buying is sold. Then we rationalize our behavior in telling ourselves that by not acting we avoided acting rashly.

Look at your procrastinating behaviors more critically to discover the true reasons for not acting. Ask yourself the following questions slowly so that you are *sure* you understand them.

When you think about changing your routine (e.g., going back to school or work, meeting new people), do you distract yourself by thinking about all the immediate things you have to do (e.g., clean the house, mow the lawn, prepare for tomorrow)?

Do you think of excuses for putting off an action that you will definitely do when conditions are right (e.g., when you get the right dress, find a little more time, or lose a few more pounds, then you will look for a job, go to school, etc.)?

When you think of doing something different, do you see yourself doing it poorly?

Do you feel confused or stupid when you begin to think of how to begin a different activity (meeting new friends, starting to exercise, learning a new hobby, embarking on a new career, etc.)?

When you think of new and exciting activities, do you dampen your enthusiasm by concentrating on the effort that they require?

If you answered yes to these questions, then you procrastinate either because you raise your feeling of anxiety by foreseeing yourself as a failure or because you prefer to drift lazily with your routine. Each of these reasons ultimately is the undoing of your happiness.

Being happy is a more accurate expression than happiness. When you use the noun "happiness," you think of something you have. Being happy, on the other hand, is an activity that is synonymous with the human functions of knowing, loving, creating, searching, seeing, wondering, respecting, and enjoying. But action always involves risk and effort. Even our routine is filled with risk. We are unaware of this truth until we are jolted by an unexpected tragedy that invades our routine. A person routinely crossing the street is hit by a car. A routine flight crashes. Even death which is expected comes unexpectedly. The fundamental cause of procrastinating is denying yourself the common-sense insight that life is spontaneous and changing. To enjoy life is to move with it. To procrastinate is to watch life pass you by.

Thinking to end thinking and thinking to begin thinking

Because the duration of our life is so uncertain, we feel vulnerable physically, emotionally, and mentally. We are always concerned about security because we know that we can lose our life and possessions in a matter of moments. The anxiety that we experience about the duration of our existence spreads to every corner of our lives. We worry about losing our money, our job, our friends, our children, our parents, our prestige, our power, our admirers, and every other thing that we think we possess. Instead of accepting the basic brittleness of human existence, we try to corral everything that we own behind the barricade of our overly cautious thinking.

We are caught between two tendencies. One tells us that life is fragile, illogical, and uncertain. The other tells us that there should be order and permanence to life. It is more comfortable to live with order and certainty. Consequently, we adopt a defensive thinking style to protect us from the anxiety that we feel when we ponder the beginning and end of our existence. We want to get rid of that fundamental anxiety quickly. There are two satisfactory answers which alleviate our feelings of insecurity—God and no God. The God answer explains the beginning and end of our existence in the ideas of creation and life everlasting. The no-God answer tells us that we begin our existence when we are born and we end our existence when we die. By choosing one or the other answer we come to terms with the fact that our earthly life is constantly slipping away. That is the way earthly life is. We cannot change it. Either God planned it that way, or no one planned it. After accepting one of these answers, we no longer bother ourselves with the ultimate question of death because either the God or the no-God answer puts the feeling of anxiety to rest. We are not concerned about the truth of the answer. Either will suffice as long as it does the job of eliminating our fears. Once we have accepted one answer or the other, then we will defend our position with our philosophical or theological arguments. Now we feel certain about our feelings, ideas, and behaviors. They all make sense, because they fit within our basic ideas about life and death.

An example of this defensive thinking is the case of Sue. Influenced by other people, Sue believes that certain people are born to do bad things because there is an evil force that seizes them at birth. Sue used to become anxious because she felt drawn to behave in a way that she wanted to avoid. Now she says that she no longer feels that anxiety because she believes that her life is controlled by an evil force. Therefore, she feels comfortable being a prostitute, although she never wanted to be one.

There are people engaged in socially accepted occupations but their thinking is similar to Sue's. They have appropriated certain ideas to justify their actions and feelings. Never again will they have to be disturbed by the fundamental questions of life and death. The big questions are nicely answered by their neat ideas. They no longer want to respond to questions about the meaning of life. They no longer want to feel the uncertainty of existence. Therefore, they bury the questions concerning the meaning of their existence under a sea of routine activities.

By thinking and behaving according to a system of ideas, you experience mental certitude and emotional security. However, you may be deceiving yourself. For example, you refuse to recognize that your marriage is crumbling, that your intellectual life is barren, that your emotional life is sterile, that your children are drifting, that work life is boring, and that your relationships with other people are false. You cannot believe that any of these things could happen to you. You have always lived according to the answers of life supplied by your religion or philosophy. In the past you found comfort in doing what you were supposed to do. Now in approaching adversity you will persist in applying these answers to make everything come out right. Instead of questioning the silent assumptions hidden behind your routine of being a wife, a husband, a father, a mother, a lover, a career person, and a human being, you prefer to practice blindly the rigid routines that you have about each of these roles. You behave this way because you want to be certain. Although you might experience the pain of confusion and alienation, nevertheless you feel comforted by knowing that you are doing what you are supposed to do. You choose to suffer some other discomfort rather than experience the pain of being uncertain about your beliefs.

When you feel uncertain about practical matters your mind operates in a definite pattern to lead you to certainty. For example, if you have reached a critical point in your career, you are confronted with the options of seeking a more challenging and rewarding position or continuing in your secure job. You begin to collect all the facts relating to the pros and cons of each decision, that is, to stay where you are or move on. Your perceptions about what you are doing and what you want to do are simply silhouetted against your most important values. Then you begin to analyze your present activities and rewards to establish a priority. You want to discover if your most important values are experienced in the rewards and activities of your current position. If you feel unsatisfied, that is, your personal values are not realized in your job function, you begin to feel uncertain about staying where you are. You start to hypothesize. You ask yourself what will you experience if you move to such and such a job. Visualizing yourself in the new job, you think about the psychological and monetary consequences of actually making the switch. Then you ask yourself if these consequences satisfy your personal values. Once you have made the logical answer, then you must make the practical decision. For example, if money is your most important value and job B offers a greater financial reward than job A, the practical decision is to move from A to B. If you do not move, then something else, which you have not admitted, is more important to you than money.

Although you might use a very pragmatic method of thinking to arrive at a decision, you might not actually make that practical decision. Why not? Thinking through the problem of remaining in your job or moving on intends to change an uncertain situation to a certain conclusion. Logically, your thinking accomplishes this objective. You may not practically follow through on your logical decision because your deepest feelings are pulling you in another direction. Your thinking, done flawlessly, functioned in a restricted area. You did not allow your mental powers to examine those silent assumptions guiding your life; consequently, the values you claim to be most important to you are in fact not the most important. You may complain that in your present job your creative powers go unused or that you do not make enough money. However, you are not willing to risk giving up what you have. Your silent assumptions are that you must be always physically and emotionally comfortable and mentally certain about the future. The feeling of security surreptitiously guides your decision more than your ideas about creativity or even your desire for more money.

The tendency to be certain can abort your best thinking. Your thoughts never give birth to productive actions. You know what is best for you, but you do not do it. You cannot jump the gap between the logical and the actual because you are afraid that in doing what you think you may lose your comfort, someone's approval or your prestige. Basically you refuse to accept the reality that your life is filled with uncertainty and novelty. Instead you prefer to construct a world around you which conforms to your unchallenged ideas. You use your thinking to rationalize your boring existence by telling yourself that you must be realistic. The translation for realistic is certain and comfortable. However, you can never eliminate the feeling of creativity lingering on the edge of your awareness.

The Art of Listening to Yourself

Dialogue 11—Taking a risk

1. Recall your irrational dependencies. In your mind list and contrast your values with your dependencies.

    For example:

Irrational Dependencies	Values
I must be successful	Freedom is important to me
I must have attention	Love is important to me

2. Recall the activities of your life in which you experience uncertainty. For example, you might be unsatisfied in your job, your marriage or your relationship with your boyfriend or girlfriend. You are not sure about continuing what you are doing.

    When you feel uncertain do you focus your attention more on your irrational dependencies than on your values?

3. Focus your attention on your values; then think about the activity of your life which concerns you. What actions do your values ask of you? For example, if loving someone and acting according to your own best judgment are important to you, can you say no to someone's unreasonable demand and risk losing the approval of that person?

12. Renewing Yourself

Did you ever use the word "creative" in your conversations and writing? Reflect for a moment on a few occasions when you spoke or wrote about creativity. Ask yourself the following questions:

In general do I speak about someone else's creativity?

Do I use the word "creative" to label the behaviors and work of other people?

When thinking and speaking about my creativity, do I always use the future tense or a subjunctive mood? For example, "I will be creative...." "If I were creative...."

If you never think and speak of your creative power and activities in the present tense, you probably are not convinced that you are creative. However, because you accept the creative actions of other people, you believe that there is some reality to the idea of creativity. But in your own case you think creativity is only a word. Even when people tell you that you are creative, you find it difficult to accept that statement on its face value, let alone all its implications. Creativity is always for the other but never for you.

If you never allow yourself to feel the new experience of your next moment of existence, you will not feel creative or behave creatively. The essence of creativity is novelty. But the most fundamental novelty is the next moment of your existence.

Sit still for a moment and concentrate on the movements of your mind-body. The next moment never was, and then suddenly you are fully aware of yourself in that next moment. You become cognizant of your personal life-force moving forward. Even before performing any external action, you can say: "I am creative." You will experience a feeling of joy when you direct your mental, emotional and physical powers to work on the world around you. When you commit yourself to express your life force through your powers of communication, you behave creatively by writing, speaking, singing, constructing, or in whatever way you make your feelings known best.

Now you know that creativity is a personal concrete life-force. It is in fact what you are, that is, a center of power to do what is important to you. Creativity is as real as you are.

You are immediately aware of certain powers. By the fact that you are questioning yourself, you know that you can think. Also by the fact that you decide what to think, you know you have the power to choose. You probably take these powers for granted. Look at them more closely. Knowing and willing are the two basic sources guiding your emotional and behavioral life. You can choose your feelings and behaviors. Through intuition you can see what is important to you, and through reason you can determine concrete ways for living your values. You can be what you see you want to be.

You may not be convinced of your creative powers. Perhaps you prefer to think that you are determined for some unknown reason to live the way that you are living. At times you may feel totally empty and powerless. You conclude that you are nothing. But you fail to realize the nonsense of that statement. To be absolutely nothing would mean not to feel anything. Ask yourself why you feel empty and powerless. You will discover that those feelings are the result of not thinking and not willing. Once you begin to think of what you want to do and then decide to do it, the feelings of emptiness and powerlessness will leave you, even before you carry out your decision externally. To know what creativity is you must experience it by exercising internal decisions. Every day you make choices. Most of your decisions, if not all, are external. For example, you choose what to eat, what to wear, where to go, what to see, or what to read. Most of these decisions are guided by external motivations, such as approval, money, success, or the requirements of the job. An internal decision is guided by an internal motive. You choose to behave in a certain way or feel a certain way because that behavior and that feeling express your chosen values. If you follow your tendencies to determine what is important, to act spontaneously, and to respond genuinely and openly to changes in and around you, you will feel and behave creatively. Each day you will create ways to achieve your goals.

You are probably impatient to experience the rewards of creativity, especially if you are always concentrating your attention on successful models. By thinking this way you can easily confuse creativity with success. Your erroneous thinking can be spotted if you put it in a syllogism.

Creativity is rewarded.
Success is rewarded.
Creativity is success.

That's like saying:

A man is an animal.
A monkey is an animal.
A man is a monkey.

If you focus on the reward you will not experience creativity. As I mentioned before, the essence of creativity is novelty. External rewards are not novel. They only appear to be new if you never had them.

Instead of looking outward toward rewards, look inward toward the sources of power, your mind and your will. There you will feel a sense of organic novelty. This feeling does not grow old with time. Throughout your entire life you can experience the feelings of novelty in the exercise of your mind and will. This experience of newness is different from the sensations you feel when you acquire a new car, a new house, a new job, a new hairdo or a new suit.

Everything around you grows old. But your powers of mind and will constantly rejuvenate themselves as long as you use them.

You can will to direct your mind to meditate about yourself. When you do, you will feel that you are a pool of energy and the director of that energy. Take a moment to recollect yourself. Think about the ideas, people or things that interest you most. Then focus your attention on what you are doing. For example, I am thinking about being free. At that point you will feel calm, peaceful, and powerful. You will feel revitalized—new.

When you experience the power of your mind and will, then you will know novelty. The experience of novelty is not having new ideas or thinking about possibilities. Human novelty is coming face to face with yourself. It is the direct experience of yourself. It is the realization that you are what you are because of yourself. Novelty is seeing that you make yourself each moment in knowing what you choose and in choosing what you know. The future or possibilities are firmly rooted in the intuitive way that you see yourself at the present moment. The intuition of yourself is the revelation of your powers to know and to choose. You are struck by the vision that you yourself are responsible for making yourself.

As you read these pages on creativity you may be saying to yourself that these ideas are absurd. They do appear strange if you are comparing them to the drudgery, routine, and monotony which you experience every day. When you feel hemmed in by the roles that you are playing—wife, husband, parent, homemaker, or bread-winner—you begin to accept the idea that reality for you is perform-ing your responsibilities in the play of life. Someone else wrote the script. Your duty is to do what you must do. If there is any time left over, then you can do what you want. To accept this attitude toward life is to make an illusion out of the reality of creativity and to make a reality out of the pantomime of routine. Each day you get up with hardly a joyful thought in your mind. You mechanically make up your face and put on your costume to meet your silent colleagues shuffling off to work. Occasionally the spell is broken by one of those crazy, creative people disrupting your routine with his or her spontaneous laughter and philosophical commentary on the absurdity of your routine.

When confronted with a different point of view about what is important in life, you begin to run a series of familiar questions through your mind.

Is life a recurring theme of doing my duty without asking any questions?

Are my behaviors, feelings, and ideas determined by my bio-logical makeup?

Have I been conditioned by my family, my education, and my religion to behave a certain way?

If you have a passive attitude toward experience, then your answer to each of these questions is "yes." Experience means what *happens* to you. You believe that the only control you have over your life is choosing to start the day by getting up in the morning. You spin the roulette wheel of life with the sound of the alarm. What happens after that depends on luck.

If you have an active attitude toward experience, then your answer to each of the above questions is "no." The very fact that you are asking questions about the meaning of life denies the statement that life is doing one's duty without questions. The tendency to question is the source of energy for developing all your powers of mind and will. Wonder, as Aristotle said, is the beginning of knowledge. It is the beginning because wonder implies a question. You wonder about the immensity and complexity of the universe. You wonder what explains its movements. You wonder about your existence. Then you wonder why you exist. To question is as human as to breathe. If you allow yourself to be frightened by these questions, you will convince yourself that too much questioning is no good. When you follow your tendency to question, you are on your way to self-discovery and creativity.

You are the most interesting reality to yourself, provided you stop taking yourself for granted. By freely pursuing the questions "Who am I?" and "Why do I exist?" you reveal to yourself your unusual mental powers. You begin to experience a feeling of yourself which begins and ends within your own consciousness. This experience is unusual because ordinarily most of your feelings about yourself start from something happening outside you. For example, you feel good about yourself because someone praised you, you feel good about yourself because you did a good job, or you feel good about yourself because you received a bonus. But you do not need these pleasant happenings to feel good about yourself. In fact, it would be impossible to feel good continuously because people on occasion criticize and reject you.

However, you can begin to know, accept, and appreciate yourself always. The first step in this learning process is to allow yourself to feel the natural curiosity about yourself which you experience in the question "Who am I?" As you question, reflect on what you are doing. You will see that you are thinking of yourself by yourself. You begin to realize that your mind is a power which can think about its own potential. If you want to think big thoughts, you can. If you want to think little thoughts, you can. If you want to think about yourself, you can. If you want to think what others think about you, you can. If you don't want to think, you can do that too. You are now aware that you can see in yourself what you want to see. Having accepted your powers of vision and choice, you are prepared to act on the world around you.

The experience of creative activity begins with internal communication which you achieved in your self-dialogue about the fundamental questions of life. Afterward, your communication extends to the world around you. Your attentiveness to nature increases your power of perception. What you took for granted—a sunrise, a sunset, a waterfall—now amazes you. Your ability to listen to other people improves with each encounter. In your conversations you reach beyond the words to see the other person's feelings and attitudes. Only after feeling the rhythm of reality in yourself, nature, and humans can you respond creatively. For example, the artist can make the colors move to his own rhythm only after he himself felt the movement of the sunset. Likewise, in all things which you want to make, listen first to yourself, then to the world around you. After sharpening your mental and physical powers, you can act creatively. You can choose to perform those behaviors which are in tune with your desires. If you want to improve your relationship with someone, you can. If you want to achieve a certain career goal, you can. If you want to feel joyful, you can. You can create, that is, make the feelings, ideas, and behaviors which you want. The fact that others have created what they wanted to do is proof that you can do the same. Also, on occasion you yourself experienced the satisfaction of seeing and choosing what you wanted. Consequently, the word "creativity" does not refer to an illusion; it signifies the kind of being you are. You are someone who can feel more than sensations, who can see more than appearances, who can choose to be more than you are.

Although you may not possess the artistic abilities of a Leonardo da Vinci or a Michelangelo, nevertheless the same creative inspiration which guided their hands is the core of your life and the center of all life. When you are in the presence of their works you can feel the spirit of their creativity touching your own desire to create. Because we all have our roots in an act of creation, we can appreciate one another's creativity. But when we deny our creative tendencies, then we feel one another's depression.

Making love creatively

Jean-Paul Sartre's play *No Exit* is performed by three characters without eyelids in a lighted room. They cannot escape each other's eyes. They feel like objects. Perhaps you feel this way when someone stares at you. When you feel possessed, you feel uncomfortable. But in regard to love is not this the case? Are you not the *object* of someone's love? Do not people in love constantly feel the conflict between being free and being possessed?

Whenever I asked adult students for the meaning of the word "love," they would smile. Usually the smile meant that you know that we know that nobody really knows what love is. Anyway, I would push and cajole them to volunteer some ideas and feelings about love. Some responses were:

"Love is a deep feeling."

"Love is the most important reality in life."

"Love means to care for someone."

"To love someone is to have understanding and compassion for that person."

"To love is to be faithful."

Then I would ask them if they loved themselves. If you apply each of the above meanings to yourself you get something else.

"Love is a deep feeling for myself."

"Love means to care for myself."

"Love is an attraction for myself."

"To love is to be faithful to myself."

When asked about the times they loved themselves most, they usually described moments when they felt free and productive. Ordinarily what they did was not monumental, but the moment was memorable because of the feelings that they were experiencing about themselves. The stories ran the gamut from sailing a boat, to planting a rose bush, to saving a life.

Then I asked them to compare the feeling of love they had for themselves with the feeling of love they had for their spouse, boyfriend or girlfriend. If they experienced the same feelings of freedom and productivity when loving someone else as when loving themselves, then they considered their love for someone else to be genuine. However, if in their love for another they felt possessive or possessed, then they experienced a contradiction. Instead of feeling free and productive they felt insecure and jealous. Obviously, to love is not to possess.

This same exercise can be used to cut loose your erroneous ideas about love. To test the meaning of love which you have for someone, begin first by reflecting on the feelings you have about yourself. See whether your dominant feelings result from following your irrational tendencies of confusion, dependence, rebellion, and skepticism or from responding to your suprarational tendencies of vision, freedom, change, and creativity. Your relationship with another person will be determined by your strongest tendencies. For example, if you tend to be dependent, then love will mean depending on someone who can satisfy your needs. If you tend to be orderly, systematized, and in control, then love will mean possessing someone. If you tend to be free and creative, then love will mean gratuitously sharing your life with someone. In proceeding this way you can root out of your life much of your emotional pain resulting from unfulfilled expectations based on your irrational ideas about love.

To answer the question "What is love?" it is necessary to ask first "Who am I?" The order in which you ask questions is essential in avoiding confusion. As you reflect on the question "Who am I?" it becomes evident that you are a thinking, choosing and feeling being. Once you have broken ground with these ideas it is not long before you feel the rumblings of your suprarational tendencies. Suddenly the ideas about yourself begin to flow.

I think
I feel
I choose
I create
I communicate
I change
I grow

Now you are ready to try love. You will know its meaning more through experience than through concepts. Just as you see yourself in an intuitive experience, so also will you recognize love. Since love escapes definition, you cannot know if you love someone by comparing the definition to the situation. Love is not a thing. Love is a changing process between two people. That is why there is so little security in love. Although your mind cannot grasp love in its concepts, yet you know it exists by the traces it leaves. If you feel free and creative in your relationship, then you know that love is in process. If you experience a feeling of anticipation about fulfilling your hopes and sharing that fulfillment, then you know that love is in process. If you feel the tension between the desire to be free and on your own and the responsibility to care for those close to you, then you know that love is in process.

Just as the feeling of freedom is the center of your life, so also it is the mark of genuine love. However, freedom and, consequently, love always involve suffering. If you want to feel free, you must be courageous enough to be yourself. That means behaving according to your values. Your decisions may invite criticism, ridicule, and at times ostracism. Even in a love relationship the partners must behave according to their convictions rather than compromise their values for the sake of comfort.

Using your intuition

If you reflect for a moment on some of your concerns and if you pay attention to ways in which your mind is operating on these concerns, you will become aware that your mind is a collection of numerous mental abilities. At one moment you may be either analyzing your experiences, synthesizing your thoughts, creatively imagining your future, meditating on your values, planning your vacation, questioning your behaviors, or validating your decisions. There are many other mental activities which you do, but you probably never take the time to distinguish one from the other. More than likely you label all these activities as "thinking." You may ask if it makes any difference in knowing your different mental activities. This is like asking the surgeon if it makes any difference what scalpel he or she uses. If you know the various activities of your mind, you will use it more efficiently and productively. You will be less confused and less emotionally upset.

Surface thinking or reflecting simply on images or appearances of reality is motivated by convenience and comfort. If you learn how to manage the people around you through your images of reality, you will experience a great deal of surface satisfaction. Knowing how to win, to compete, and to be number one depends on your arsenal of self-images and on your skillful and timely use of them. However, you must protect yourself from your questioning tendencies. Asking what you are competing for, what you are winning, and what you are number one at is not cricket in this gamesmanship.

When you allow yourself the freedom to pursue the answers to some fundamental questions about the meaning of today's existence, you discover through your intuitional thinking that you are more than the images of yourself. Intuition is your primary and most powerful mental activity accounting for your self-awareness and your penetrating perceptions of the world around you. The following diagram represents the relationship among intuition, reason, perception, behavior and the external world.

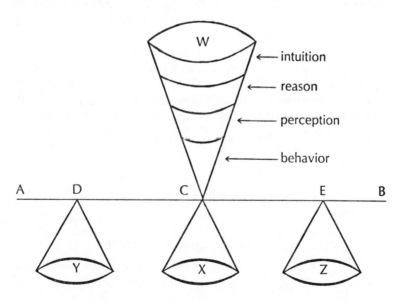

Plane AB represents the world in which you act. Points D, C, E, etc., represent your particular behaviors. Cone W is you. Cones X, Y, Z, etc., are other people. As you can see, your intuition and that of others is open-ended. The effectiveness of your behavior, the sharpness of your perception, and the appropriateness of your reason depend on the content of your intuition. For example, if you see yourself as someone choosing your own values in life, then your reasoning, perception, and behavior will be profoundly influenced by your deep feeling of freedom. When you respond to others at points C, D, E, etc., you realize that these encounters reveal only a part of yourself and those persons.

Your intuitive power has always been present in your life, but you can recall instances when it was most operative. During those moments you willed to concentrate your powers of sensation and mind on yourself or on a prized reality outside you. You became vividly aware of certain aspects of yourself or of your chosen object. For example, you may have become sharply conscious of your body, your mental processes, a tree, or other objects. At one moment you felt that you were in what you saw. You could feel the movement of the waterfall, the power of the sunset, the ecstasy of the musician, the exhilaration of the triumphant sportsman, and the satisfaction of the successful businessman. In each of these experiences you maintained your identity because you were fully aware that it was you who were experiencing something. Through your efforts to see and feel all you can in yourself and others, you kept the experience alive. Because you were conscious of the fact that you could choose to focus your attention elsewhere, you became aware that you were a person who could direct your mental and physical powers. You intuitively saw yourself as a free person.

The Art of Listening to Yourself

Dialogue 12—Creating yourself

Goal setting is a major activity of the creative and happy person. When your objectives are clear and reachable, you feel enthusiastic about everything you do and exhilarated by each action bringing you closer to the realization of what you want.

Use the diagram below to discover what prevents you from feeling like a full person in all your activities.

What values will help you feel like yourself in all your activities?

Make your values concrete by deciding on specific feelings, behaviors and achievements that you will practice now.

A. Summary of Not Being Me

Activity	Irrational Dependencies	Unwanted Feelings	Unwanted Behaviors	Unwanted Results
Parent				
Spouse				
Lover				
Worker				
Behavior				
Friend				
Student				
Daughter				
Son				

B. Summary of Being Me

Activity	Values	Desired Feelings	Positive Behaviors	Desired Achievements
Parent				
Spouse				
Lover				
Worker				
Believer				
Friend				
Student				
Daughter				
Son				

Part Five

LIFE IS WORTH
THE EFFORT IF YOU KNOW
HOW TO LIVE IT

13. The Mental Road to Self-Destruction

Lynn was pursuing her bachelor's degree at a metropolitan university. Plagued with financial difficulties and loneliness, she decided to live with her boyfriend completing his degree. It was the perfect solution, she felt, since two can live cheaper than one, and two can keep each other company. Besides, she said, "we love each other." Neither had a clear idea about a career goal, a long-term love relationship, children, or where they wanted to live and work. But they did feel a spell of relief from their confusion brought on by financial.stress and loneliness. They felt comforted by each other's presence. After eight months the cracks in their relationship were beginning to show. Two months later the debacle occurred. He moved out and once again she was alone and stuck with the rent. Lynn dropped out of school. Within three months she hooked up with another guy holding a steady job. The scenario repeated itself. After a year the relationship crumbled and Lynn was left with the bills. Her next strategy was to move in with two girls her own age. Within five months the two girls split. Lynn was now saddled with the rent for a three-bedroom apartment. The second boyfriend, who had walked out on her, called to see if they could patch up their differences. "The future is looking bright," she thought. He came back to her, and they shared the three-bedroom apartment. Within four months he decided to quit his job because

Lynn had landed a well-paying job. Now he would be able to take the time to search for a rewarding career. The search lasted for a year without any results. Once again they severed their relationship. Lynn decided to take a studio apartment and live by herself. She discovered that she was pregnant, and after a month of indecision she opted for an abortion. Within a couple of months she had her health, an apartment, and a good job. She was ready to return to school, but she felt she needed a close relationship with someone. Once again the second boyfriend showed up. Now employed, he moved in with Lynn. After one month he quit his job to search for that rewarding career. Six months later, and still with no job, they decided to part.

For approximately four years, Lynn was riding an emotional scenic railway. She complained that she was unhappy because people put her through too many changes. Sitting alone in her sparsely furnished studio she sank into the pits of depression. She did not want to feel depressed. After thinking about the past four years, she came to the conclusion that the actions of other people made her depressed. She vowed that she would not get close to anyone anymore.

Let's review Lynn's story in slow motion so that we can accurately label her behaviors and thinking.

1. She was pursuing a bachelor's degree, a boyfriend, and money. She was having difficulties getting all three at the same time.

Lynn was *confused*.

When asked what was most important to her, she hesitated a long time before answering, "I really don't know." Her ignorance about herself was not due to a lack of ideas about love, marriage, careers, and a dozen other topics. Conversing about any of these subjects as an objective spectator of life, she made eminent sense. Most of her peers respected her opinions. In fact, she was elected class representative to the student government. Although she was intellectually and socially proficient, she was ineffective in managing her own life. Because she did not determine her priorities in life, she wandered aimlessly in and out of "love" relationships. She had no clear-cut goals concerning her personal development, her relationships with men and her career. She was like a powerful ship riding the high seas with no destination.

To be confused is to be mixed up. The word comes from the Latin *confundere* which means to pour in together. Now picture your mind as a container into which you pour your ideas and experiences about life. Then shake the container. Without question you will feel confused. Having a bundle of ideas and experiences about life does not get you out of your confusion. The ideas are only the tools helping you to arrive at your destination. Before you can make your ideas work for you, you have to know where you are going and what you want in life. But only you can decide what you want. Unless you choose what is important to you, you will be confused.

2. Lynn escaped the pain of being confused by depending on other people to give her comfort.

Lynn was looking for a way out of her confusion. Instead of depending on her powers of mind and will to give her direction, she depended on someone else to give her comfort. When she experienced the warmth of her boyfriend's attention, then her life was good. When he left her, then her life was bad. The meaning of her life hung on her boyfriend's behavior. When he moved on, she fell.

If you have no personal goal in life, such as to improve yourself intellectually and professionally or to improve yourself emotionally by growing in patience, assertiveness, and joy, then what do *you* live for each day? Without a clear goal you will spend each day trying to avoid aggravation by seeking a few simple pleasures. Soon you will become dependent on someone, something, or some activity for your comfort. If you find a minimum amount of satisfaction in surrendering yourself to your job, your home responsibilities, your wife, your husband, your children, your boyfriend, your girlfriend, your friends or your negative addictions, you will not feel the need to think about your personal goals. The meaning of life becomes doing what you have to do without being annoyed.

3. After several emotional flops, Lynn became angry. "Nobody cares for me. Nobody is loyal to me. If that bum tries to come back to me, I'll make his life miserable."

Lynn was *rebelling* against those people on whom she had depended.

When you think that your survival is threatened, you get

angry. You want to destroy the invader. However, ninety percent of your anger is caused by an imaginary invader. When you allow yourself to become ninety percent dependent on someone or some activity for your happiness, then you have created a potential invader. If you lose a job, a friend, a lover, a wife, or a husband, you get angry. "They should not do *this* to me." *This* means robbing you of your happiness. But look closely at the sequence of your behaviors. No one robbed you of anything. You gave away your power to be happy by allowing yourself to become dependent. When you choose to get married, to take a particular job, and to have children, you do not simultaneously choose to stop thinking for yourself. But, as the days pass, it becomes easier not to think, and not to be authentically responsible. Living becomes *having* a family, a boyfriend, or a job. But living is not *having*. Living is choosing to be with whom *you* want to be and to do what *you* want. Unless you make a daily mental effort to see this difference, you will not avoid being pulled into dependency.

4. After venting her anger, Lynn became tired. "I can't trust anyone, even myself. All those great ideas I had about life are not true." She began to withdraw from people. She viewed everyone *skeptically*.

When Lynn was four years younger, she felt confused because she had doubts about what she wanted. She never cleared up those doubts by finding out what was important to her. Now, after her negative experiences, her doubt runs much deeper. She asks herself whether there is anything important in life. The answer for her is "no." Her only purpose in life is to avoid getting hurt. Consequently, she will not become dependent on anyone anymore.

Once Lynn rejected dependency, she was in a critical position. If she became skeptical about her own mental and volitional powers to guide her life effectively, then she would sink into depression. If she explored her doubts about the meaning of life with some confidence in her power of reason, she would establish some order in her emotional life. Basically, she asked if she could find *within herself* reasons for living. Asking this question is the first step on the road to self-control. She chose to examine her past to see how she had been thinking. In fact, she was reviewing her past to discover what philosophy of life she had, if any. She was determined to construct a system of positive ideas to guide her life. Happily, Lynn turned her life around.

Having flirted with the idea of suicide, she averted it because she began to reflect on her own thinking. She saw two exits from the dungeon of depression. One was death; the other was thought. She decided to go out through thought. "Poor thinking got me in here; proper thinking will get me out." She compared her limited ways of thinking in the past to her broader thinking capacities in the present.

1. Appearances

Lynn was always dazzled by appearances. Her judgment of other people was based on how they looked and how they entertained her. Because she had not established any inner life of her own, she could not perceive the selfish intentions of other people.

Using her intuitive powers, she clearly saw that thinking independently and pursuing her career goals were more important to her than the passing comforts which she received in her romantic relationships. She still wanted a close relationship with a man, but now she judged the quality of his total personality before being swept off her feet by her desire for attention.

You probably have experienced the same tendency of throwing your better judgment to the wind for some immediate comfort. Recall an incident and review your thinking during that incident in slow motion. The following questions will help you discover your thought patterns:

Was I greatly *impressed* or overpowered by what I saw, felt, or heard?

Did I want to let myself be taken by what I saw, felt, or heard?

Was my mind filled with images in which I was identified with what I saw, felt, or heard?

If your answer to each of these questions is "yes," and if you chose to behave on only the information from this type of thinking, then in time you will be confused. You expect great happiness by *having* what you see, feel, or hear; when this expectation is not realized, you ask, "What happened?" You complain, "I was so happy with what I saw, but now I'm so miserable with what I got."

Your confusion is caused by your shallow thinking. You deluded yourself. Reality is more than what you see, feel, or hear. Were you ever fooled by jumping into water over your head when you thought it was shallow? Appearances are deceptive.

You can avoid the grief of confusion by developing good judgment. Begin by concentrating on what is important to you. Then analyze what you see, feel, and hear in the light of your own personal values. The more you decide to behave according to your own values, the more you will become your own person.

2. Romanticism

Lynn dreamed of a future free from conflict and effort. She desired a man who would shower her with the affection and attention that she had never had. In each of her relationships she behaved as if her dream had come true. She refused to see the limitations of her partner. She ignored the practical problems such as not having enough money to pay the bills. She forgot her educational and career goals. All her efforts were spent on avoiding reality so that she could convince herself that her dream was coming true.

Instead of thinking about how her relationship should be, Lynn began to accept how in fact it was. She realized that she was living a double life. Externally, she pretended to be happy. Internally, she knew that she was dejected. As the contrast between her behavior and her feelings sharpened, she approached the breaking point. She had to accept her feelings as true or continue to make her dream come true. Giving up her romanticism, she began to ask herself why she felt so frustrated. It seemed that all her efforts to be happy returned only sadness. She realized that her emotional pain was the result of allowing her happiness to depend on someone else. "Happiness is not receiving attention and affection from someone. I am happy when I'm doing what is important to me." Her internal conversations began to make sense because she was paying attention to her common-sense intuitions, such as:

I am responsible for my own feelings.

I choose my own goals.

I am free to think about myself the way I want.

I'm not dependent on other people's attention to feel good about myself.

To live is always to begin. The end of one phase of life is the beginning of something new.

When you give yourself exclusively to romantic thinking, you become emotionally dependent on your heroes or ideals. You are looking for some charismatic person or some ideal way of living which will save you from drowning in your confusion. If some respectable person or idea catches your attention, you embellish its power and their attractiveness. Then you convince yourself that your world will be better because you have found the ideal person or the secret formula to the meaning of life. Following your irrational tendency to be emotionally and mentally dependent on someone or some idea increases your confusion instead of eliminating it. You expect someone or some idea to make you happy, but your happiness is your commitment to your vision of life. As long as you wait for happiness to come from someone or something outside yourself, you will be baffled.

3. Dogmatism

You will experience a good deal of friction if you behave according to your set ideas about the way the world should be. Lynn was constantly trying to fit people, events, and herself into her own ideas, but most of her ideas began in negation and ended in perfection. For example, she was confused in her relationships with men because she could not sensibly respond to the reality that people are always changing. There will always be misunderstandings between two growing people. She chose to deny that reality by saying, "Men should not be insensitive to my needs for affection and attention." Once she denied the limitations of human beings, then she expected them to behave the way they should behave—perfectly. It is obvious that Lynn was headed for frustration.

Lynn gave up the idea of creating and living in an imaginary world. Instead of denying and rebelling against the inconsistencies, misunderstandings, and insensitivity of other people, she simply recognized them. She also realistically appraised the positive traits of other people as well as her own. Her common-sense perspective on the abilities and limitations of human beings helped her to behave more effectively with other people. Because her expectations of herself and other people were shaped by her analytic thinking, she no longer felt a raging anger when people crossed her, or depression when people rejected her.

If you get angry often, analyze your thinking process. You will discover that you get angry when you or other people violate your ideas about the way the world should be. That world may be your home, your office, your social life, your religion, your community, or your country. Your indignation and irresponsible anger are smoke screens covering up your weakness, which is dependency. You are really saying, "If the world were right, I would feel good." Instead of accepting the responsibility for your own happiness, you prefer to appear strong by vociferously complaining about everything that goes wrong. You are more courageous and productive when you accept the world the way it is. If you see yourself the way you are, you will discover that you can live effectively in the world the way it is.

4. Generalizing

Many times you have probably said:
"All men are like that."
"All women are like that."
"Nothing ever goes right for me."
"All politicians are corrupt."
"I'll never be happy."

These statements are absolute condemnations of yourself and other people. You are serving yourself a life sentence to the penitentiary of pessimism and misery when you generalize each of your negative experiences into sweeping negative judgments about yourself and everyone else. It is so easy to do. When someone has hurt you, you tend to doubt the goodness of people in general.

After generalizing her negative experiences, Lynn became skeptical about everyone's intentions toward her. She believed that people were only using her. Her skeptical reaction to people was entirely consistent with her dogmatic view about the way life should be. When people did not behave in the way she thought that they should, she no longer trusted them. After investing so much effort and hope in trying to make her dream relationship come true and after being rejected by those who she thought loved her, she was faced with the choice either of believing that love is not possible or of changing her ideas about the meaning of love.

Just as the pattern of each snowflake is different, so also each human personality is different. But the mind has a tendency to put our experiences in groups. It also has a tendency to recognize the individual differences of each experience. However, we find that it is easier to generalize our experiences and forget the individual differences. For example, you may have three or more children. You try to treat them all the same. You can think of many examples in which people consider themselves to be fair because they behave equally toward everyone. When your teacher does not behave the way all teachers are supposed to behave, when your husband does not behave the way all husbands are supposed to behave, when your boss does not behave the way all bosses are supposed to behave, or when your girlfriend does not behave the way all girlfriends are supposed to behave, you complain that you are being treated unfairly. As long as you expect people to behave according to their roles instead of their individual personalities, you will be disappointed in them. After several unfulfilled expectations, you begin to lose hope in everyone.

One day Lynn was sitting on a lawn in the park. She was gazing at the grass. Little by little each blade of grass came into focus for her. "They all look the same, but one blade is different from the next," she thought. It was a simple thought. The fact that blades of grass and even people are different from one another is a reality that she had taken for granted. However, the uncomparability of each human being is a reality that requires all her attention if she wants to know a single human being. She began to realize that she never really knew anyone. Instead, she was always looking for someone to play the part of the responsible, tender, and caring lover—a part for which she wrote the script. When no one was good enough to play the role, then no one was any good. Once Lynn was aware that her negative feelings of anger, hostility, and depression were actually a result of her irrational thinking patterns, she decided to practice rational ways of thinking such as seeing differences among people and not expecting more than what someone can give.

Instead of complaining how everyone is unfair to her, she marvels at the differences and consequently the novelty in the world.

14. Mental Strategies for Self-Profit

Take a moment one day to stand aside and watch the flow of people filing into the subways and buses, bustling about the office, rushing through the streets, milling about the park, browsing through the shopping centers, driving their cars, or doing a hundred and one other activities which seem to tell you that these people are on their way to get something.

Ask yourself, "What makes them move about?" "What are they going for?" If you don't know the answers, then join the ranks of moving masses and ask yourself the same questions.

Each day you get up and move about—maybe to work, to school, or around the house. But every day you put yourself in motion. What makes you move about? It seems like a ridiculous question, because the answer seems so obvious. What are some answers? "I move about because that's the way life is." "There are things I must do every day." You can become more specific if you give more thought to the question. Your answers might be similar to the following:

"I want to keep my job."

"I want to make money."

"I want to keep the house in order."

"I want a professional diploma."

"I want to play."

Reflect more by following each answer with the question "Why?" For example, why do you want to keep your job? Your answer might be one or several of the following:

"I need security."

"I need the satisfaction which comes from work."

"I need to keep busy.."

"I need the prestige which comes from the job."

The list could be continued. The point is that you are saying that you move about to satisfy a need. Ultimately, the purpose for all your motion is your own self-profit. When you feel that you are achieving something which you thought that you were missing, then you feel satisfied. Self-profit or self-interest for you means fulfilling your felt needs.

Continue to reflect on your felt needs by asking yourself what you mean when you say:

"I want to get something out of this marriage."

"I want to get enough money from this job."

"I want to get satisfaction from this career."

"I want a satisfying home life."

The meaning of these statements refers to the basic desire of feeling good about yourself. Theoretically, you might believe that you *are* good, even if you are without money, love, and a career. But, practically, you *feel* good or satisfied only when you *have* what you want.

However, just *having* money, a good job, and a pleasant home life is not enough to make you feel good. Many people have these things yet they do not feel satisfied with themselves. When you *want* what you have, then you are content. But rarely do you want something just to have it. Usually you want something for another reason. If you examine the hidden reasons behind your possessions you will discover that you really want to feel something internally. That something can be independence, recognition, peace, comfort, love, or some other internal feeling.

How to get what you want

If you deeply want to feel good about yourself, but you believe that there is no way to achieve this goal, then you will feel frustrated and eventually depressed. On the other hand, if you pay attention to your common sense telling you that you are a rational being who solves problems, then you will look for ways to satisfy your desire for a feeling of well-being. The first step toward achieving your self-interest is to observe yourself and your environment carefully. What you observe is determined by what you want most. For example, if you believe having money will give you the type of *security* you want, then you assess yourself in terms of your marketable attributes. Next, you channel your attention to the business which matches your strengths. Once you have determined the boundaries of your career world, then you observe in detail the rules and the success stories of that world.

You will begin to observe connections among events. For example, people with highly developed social skills generally make more money than people who are smart but retiring. You begin to recognize that certain patterns of behavior are usually followed by the same results. The more you observe yourself, the more you will recognize that your patterns of behavior have certain effects on other people. You begin to ask yourself which behaviors will get me what I want. By asking this question you are following your rational tendency which seeks to put order into situations. The particular order that you want to discover is the cause-effect relationships in your career world. You want to know what causes people to be successful. More particularly, you want to know how you should direct your ideas and behaviors to achieve the results that you want.

After having observed and analyzed yourself and your work world, you construct a plan of action. Your game-plan is really a theory of how to succeed in your career. You believe in your theory because it is based on the concrete evidence collected from your observations. Your next step is to set up timetables to achieve a series of intermediate goals. Each success reinforces your belief in what you are doing. You begin to taste the *security* which you want so much. Each increase in salary is a step closer to your final goal.

Occasionally you might fall short of your immediate goal. However, you have confidence in your mental ability to diagnose and rectify the problem. After a short delay you are on your way.

To get what you want, you must first believe that you can control not only your behavior but the consequences of your behavior. That is, you must believe that you can actually make happen what you want to happen. Secondly, you must know *how* to achieve what you want.

Learning how to get what you want depends on how well you pay attention to your rational tendency of putting order in your life. Once you see the cause-effect relationships of your behavior, you can choose to strengthen the behaviors which give you the results that you want. If you think that you will be rewarded for behaving assertively and you actually are rewarded with a promotion, then you have learned that assertiveness is an effective way of behaving to advance your career.

In the foregoing example the major consequence was feeling secure. Getting money was the means to feel good about yourself. But as I said before, feeling good about yourself is an internal activity. Possessions do not *make* you feel good. You feel good because you *want* what you have. You can learn *how* to get things. But do you know *what* you want?

Knowing what you want

Often we assume that we know what we want. The following section of an interview illustrates this point.

Counselor: At this point in your life, what do you want?
Client: I want an exciting career. Not a nine to five drag.
Counselor: Like what?
Client: Like being an actor. I've got the talent. I've got the motivation. I really want it, but I'm not making any headway in getting it.
Counselor: You strongly believe you can become an accomplished actor.
Client: I know I can.
Counselor: What do you want from being an actor?
Client: Have you ever been to the theater?
Counselor: Many times.
Client: Then you can imagine how the performers feel at the end of the play when they take their curtain calls. That's what I want.

The client began by saying that he wanted to be an actor. He ended by saying that he wanted the feeling that comes with the audience's applause. Wanting to be an actor is a clearly definable goal. The achievement of that goal requires basic talents and learned skills. However, the feeling that comes with the audience's approval is not clearly seen by the client. He has simply assumed that feeling good about himself will be the consequence of feeling approved, and feeling approval will be caused by acting.

Confusing external and internal goals is a common source of disappointment. How often have you worked at achieving a better relationship with someone or at producing a better product but did not get the feelings you wanted? Either you were not clear in your own mind about the particular feeling you expected, or you assumed that the achievement of certain external goals always pays off with self-satisfying feelings.

For example, if you believe that having an abundance of money is equal to feeling secure, you might be deceived. Before striving after external goals you need to clarify your understanding of security. On the surface you might be assuming that money gives you emotional security as well as financial stability. Usually, the fault of not clearly knowing what you want is your failure to distinguish internal goals from external goals. This mistake can generate many self-defeating behaviors. Another case in point is the person who believes that he can feel good about himself, only if he has a rewarding relationship with a particular person. If the relationship doesn't work out, the person falls apart emotionally, and sometimes physically. The following example illustrates this point.

Bill was a "well-adjusted" young man with a graduate degree, a good job, and a bright future. His marriage to Joan was the centerpiece of his ideal life. He felt good when he stood back and looked at what he had. He was like the man gazing at the enormous Kodak photo gracing the entire wall of the lobby of Grand Central Station in New York City. Frequently this photo depicts an outdoor scene of the young American family posed against a comfortable house nestled in the arms of nature. For Bill, that picture represented his entire life. However, little by little Joan began to fade from the picture. One day she left Bill. The picture was ruined and so was the man looking at it. He believed that he had lost the meaning to his life. His work performance and his health declined. At one time Bill was the model of the successful man. He knew how to get the things that he wanted, and he got them. However, he made the mistake of assuming that feeling good about himself was the effect of having things that he wanted. Self-interest is not that easily satisfied.

Listing your internal and external goals is a useful exercise. You might object to do this by saying, "Don't bother me with that nonsense. I know what I want." Your problems, like those of most of us human beings, begin when you take too much for granted. You believe that you know your own mind. You believe that you are doing what you really want to do. If you look closely at your thinking and behavior you will probably discover that you spend most of your thinking time trying to justify, rationalize, or figure out your behavior. If this is the case, then you do not know what you want.

Look at the following lists of some internal and external goals. If you do not find your goals there, add them. Then ask yourself the following questions:

1. Which goals are most important to me now? List them in order of importance.
2. Is your number one goal an internal or external goal?
3. Which external goals match my internal goals?
4. Does the achievement of my external goals cause the fulfillment of my internal goals, or does the achievement of my internal goals cause the achievement of my external goals?

(1) Internal goals

To feel independent. To feel that I am making my own decisions about what I will do.

To feel comfortable. To feel that I am enjoying the pleasures of life.

To feel successful.

To feel worthwhile.

To feel wanted by other people.

To feel that I am useful and productive.

To feel deeply loved.

To feel that I am maturing mentally and emotionally.
To feel creative.
To feel powerful.

(2) External goals
    To have a prestigious job.
    To have a very active sex life.
    To accumulate an abundance of money.
    To have a service career.
    To have many friends.
    To have a variable and active social life.
    To have an intellectual career.
    To have prestigious friends.
    To have power over other people.
    To have an understanding and caring husband or wife.
    To have children.
    To achieve something concrete. (To get a degree; to build my own house; to reach a new sales record for myself; to get a promotion; to have my own business.)

Answering the chicken and the egg question—are internal goals achieved before external goals or vice versa?—will demand plenty of thought. Suppose feeling worthwhile is your number one internal goal. Next to feeling worthwhile you might have listed the external goals of having a prestigious job, having a caring husband or wife, and having many friends. Do you feel worthwhile because you have the prestigious job, or do you get the prestigious job because you project your feeling of self-worth? The more that you think about the relationship between internal and external goals, it will become clear to you that you need to achieve your internal goals before satisfying your external goals.

If you say to yourself that you really do not know what you want, then you have not decided what is important to you. No matter how well you can use the rational method to achieve external goals, that method of observing, analyzing, hypothesizing, and checking your results cannot tell you what is important to you. The rational method of thinking helps you to live out what is important to you.

The question of importance is a question of value. Some people believe that their values are learned from other people. Others believe that their values depend on the situations in which they find themselves. Neither position explains how you know what is of value to you. You *immediately* know what is of worth to you. For example, knowing and choosing are two activities which are important to you. Without these activities you are not you. These activities *are* your worth. You can intuitively grasp the values of knowing and choosing.

As you learn how to reason, you begin to derive other values from the ones you know intuitively. For example, knowing more about yourself and other people may be valuable because you simply want to know more. You may want to know more about yourself to make better behavioral choices. However, when you decide that feeling independent is an important internal goal, you are expressing in a rational and emotional way what you already know intuitively. You know that you can think whatever you please. If you want to think of yourself as worthless, you can. Or if you want to think of yourself as a person of worth, you can. No matter what you think, you are thinking independently of other people and situations. Once you are aware of your independent thinking, you begin to realize the power of your mind. You can choose what you will think and what will be of value to you. As you decide on your values, you will be deciding on your internal goals.

You do not get what you want because you do not think realistically. Before going any further let's take a closer look at the word "realistic." The word "real" can mean different things to different people. How many times have people called you unrealistic, while you, in your own mind, were calling *them* unrealistic? You have these breakdowns in communication because you believe that what you are thinking about in your mind really exists outside your mind. For example, a father may think of his teenage daughter as an underachieving and consequently a lazy student. But the daughter sees herself as someone who is always asking questions to learn more about herself. Her attitude toward learning might not produce the high grades that her father expects from her. Consequently, the father is constantly after his daughter to do what she is supposed to do because he believes his daughter is a lazy person. In reality his daughter is not achieving not because she is lazy, but because she does not know how to organize her time. The father behaves inappropriately toward his daughter because he has an unrealistic idea of her.

Not only do you have a problem communicating with others because you see reality differently than they do, but you also have difficulty talking with yourself for the same reason. You have different ideas about yourself. "Which idea of myself is really me?" you ask. There is a long series from which you can choose.

"Am I consistent or inconsistent?"

"Am I sociable or unsociable?"

"Am I smart or average?"

"Am I considerate or inconsiderate?"

"Am I assertive or shy?"

"Am I courageous or fearful?"

To have a real picture of yourself means to have a clear and comprehensive idea of yourself which is based not only on your past performances but also on your present values. A realistic idea of yourself *simultaneously* includes your strong and weak points. The key word is simultaneously. Take a moment to review your values and your actions within the past month. Label your positive qualities which helped you to carry out your values and your negative traits which blocked you from doing what was important to you. You might have something like the following:

Value = Caring for your wife and children

Positive traits	Negative traits
Industrious—repaired children's toys; fixed wife's kitchen equipment	*Inattentive*—watched ballgame instead of answering wife's question
Giving—took kids to circus; did errands for wife	*Impatient*—put off kids' questions
Thoughtful—put money in savings for children's education	

Follow the same procedure for your five most important values. After you have completed the exercise you will have a realistic view of yourself. You can achieve what you want only after you know who you are.

Focus your attention on the qualities that you like most about yourself. At the same time, keep an eye on your glaring deficiencies. Now, with this realistic view of yourself take a second look at your values. In the example above, caring for his family is a very important activity for this particular father, but he fails to communicate with them. It is time for him to change. When he tells himself that he is living up to his value because he does so many things for them, he is fooling himself. He is not speaking to himself from a realistic understanding of himself. On the other hand, if he believes that he has failed completely in carrying out his value because he has not spent time speaking to his wife and children about things which interest them, again he is fooling himself. The real him is a mixture of pluses and minuses. He can experience satisfaction in the achievement of all his values only after he develops a realistic understanding of himself.

Self-profit is achieving what is valuable and important to *you*. It is reasonable, then, that you know more about *you*. Unless you begin by knowing who you are, you can easily deceive yourself about your self-profit. Some people believe that *they are* what *they have*. Self-profit for these people means collecting more pleasure, more money, or more security. If they lose what they have, then they lose themselves. True self-profit is based on a knowledge of yourself. Knowledge of yourself is the most enduring and easily attained value.

The reward for knowing yourself

Nature has a way of building on the positive and eliminating the negative. Even though you are distracted in a thousand ways from knowing yourself, nevertheless self-knowledge is a natural tendency. The more you become insightful about yourself, the more you get a behavioral grip on yourself. You become more self-directed and assertive in your actions as you increase your self-knowledge.

When your values are clear and when you have a realistic understanding of yourself, then you know what you want. You get what you want by behaving assertively. Behaving assertively begins by thinking assertively. No longer are your self-statements full of might's, should's, maybe's, and if's. You speak to yourself in short, crisp, declarative sentences. For example, "I want a promotion, so I will study for an advanced degree," instead of, "If I can get an advanced degree, maybe I'll get a promotion."

When you clearly know *what* you want and *how* to get it, you will speak with authority and determination. Your speech will be a clear reflection of your organized thoughts. You will not feel embarrassed to voice your ideas. You will not mumble or gobble your words. You will not hedge what you want to say. Your speech will be strong and to the point.

When you are clear about who you are and what you want, you carry yourself energetically. You give off rays of contagious enthusiasm. You move with vigor and a sense of direction. In contrast, the person who does not know himself usually looks lost and weighed down by the world.

The reward for knowing yourself is the enjoyment you receive in doing what is important to you. Many people do not experience the joy of living because they do not know *how* to achieve what is important to them. For example, loving someone and being loved is important to all people. Yet, how many feel permanently loved? And how many believe that they *can* love?

The first step in learning how to get what you want is knowing yourself. Your unfulfilled goal is the result of not knowing yourself. You can learn *how* to realize your goals only after you begin to know your own mind. Common sense will tell you that you have to know what something is before you know what it can do. The same principle applies to yourself.

How many times did you catch yourself scolding yourself for not doing what you know you could have done? You *knew* what you wanted to do, but you did not do it. The following story illustrates the point.

Whenever Mary had a meeting with her boss she became anxious. She wanted a raise in salary. Her competence warranted an increase in pay. However, her boss, for reasons of his own, was critical of her performance from time to time, but on the whole he begrudgingly agreed that she performed well. Mary had a great supply of self-confidence in relation to her work, but she felt threatened in the presence of an authority figure. Intellectually, she knew her career goals and the ways to achieve them. She also had a good understanding of herself. She was aware of her irrational ideas concerning authority figures. After rejecting the idea that she could not overcome her anxiety, she accepted the idea that she was producing her own fears by not thinking correctly. She started to put her positive ideas to practice. Her objective was to speak assertively to her boss about her raise. One evening she rehearsed all her arguments. The following day she would ask her boss for a meeting. The next morning, before she got a chance to initiate a meeting, her boss said that he wanted to see her after work. The rest of her day was filled with anxiety. She wondered what she had done wrong now. At the meeting the boss talked about some trivial matters. Mary did not do what she wanted—namely, to present her arguments for a raise. That evening in her quiet moments she started kicking herself for not carrying out her intention.

Mary failed to do what she wanted because she broke her concentration. When her boss asked to see her after work, she let go of her concrete intention and focused on the boss's possible intentions. If she had paid attention to her own mind at the moment the boss asked to see her after work, she would have responded, "Very good. I have an important matter to discuss with you. See you at five." By being assertive from the start she would have avoided those feelings of anxiety.

Although knowing yourself is important, it is not enough. You may be very aware of your positive and negative tendencies, your past performances, your attitudes, your values, and your goals. However, living means to put the knowledge of yourself into practice. The bridge between knowledge of self and practice is decision-making.

Let us return to the example of Mary to illustrate how decision-making works. The evening before going to work Mary reviewed what was important to her. She chose a particular way of seeing herself in relation to her boss—namely, as one adult to another. Doing what she chose would have been the fulfillment of the decision. She did not complete this decision because she interrupted her own rhythm by letting herself slip into another way of looking at her boss. At the moment her boss asked to see her after work, she focused her attention on the possible reasons and consequences of that meeting. On the previous evening she had her own reasons and projected consequences for that meeting. The knowledge she had of herself and her goals would have been carried out in practice if she had focused on the choice that she had made the previous evening—namely, to see herself as one adult before another adult. If she had concentrated on the choice of seeing herself as an adult at the moment her boss spoke to her, she would have behaved differently.

Let us use another example to demonstrate the crucial point where a decision becomes an action. Suppose you decide to lose weight. You choose a particular way of looking at certain foods. For example, starches and sweets are no good. If you begin to tell yourself that a sweet now and then will not have tremendous consequences, you begin to lose concentration. Instead of focusing on your choice to view sweets negatively, you begin to bargain about the relative weight-producing effects of some sweets. At that moment you let go of your original decision, and, instead, you decide to haggle over the amount of calories in sweets. You will eat a sweet. Then you will justify your action by telling yourself that you ate the sweet with the lowest calorie count. In reality you broke the rhythm of your original decision which was not to eat sweets.

Doing what you know and what you want requires *concentration*. Daily reflection on your values and your goals builds up your concentration. It is impossible to foresee and control all the various and spontaneous situations during the day. However, you can control your own ideas. Your alert and self-directed mind is superior to any situation.

Thinking your way to self-profit

In a world of a thousand daily distractions and pressures, concentration seems to be a difficult personal quality to master. Learning *how* to concentrate is easy. *Doing* what you intellectually learn demands more self-discipline. The difficulty in concentrating is getting rid of all your excuses for not concentrating. Have you ever complained that life has no meaning while at the same time you refuse to center your attention on what is important to you? The assumption underlying your complaint is that the world should find you something to make your life meaningful. You see yourself as an empty cup, waiting to be filled. You will wait forever. Self-profit is the result of self-responsibility and self-knowledge. Your knowledge becomes practical when you concentrate.

As you are concentrating you are injecting what is most important to you into your daily behavior. To illustrate this point picture yourself as a surgeon. Your knowledge of medicine is funneled to a thousand little actions. As a surgeon you are centering yourself between what you know and the situation in front of you. You focus your attention on the knowledge you need in order to perform as an excellent surgeon. You apply the same thinking process when you want to perform as an excellent person. You concentrate, that is, you direct your attention to what is most important to you, and then you funnel these values into your daily actions. Just as the surgeon has to learn and practice certain mental activities, so also you have to learn the correct mental activities which lead to self-profit.

I. What to avoid

Avoid the following mental attitudes:

1. "Someday I'll get lucky and I'll get what I want."
2. "I wish I had done things differently in the past."
3. "I wish I could live and work somewhere else where the people and the environment are more pleasant."
4. "Eventually things will get better."

Each of the above statements, and any others like them, are excuses for not accepting your responsibility to think in detail about your values and your everyday actions. Some people believe that getting what they want happens automatically as they grow older. They believe that happiness is inherited. When they feel that they are not getting their fair share, they become hostile and angry. But they themselves suffer most from their irrational ideas and behavior.

II. What to practice

1. Accept yourself as you are and the world as it is.

The first step in changing yourself and the world is accepting both as they are. Acceptance of yourself means allowing your behavior, beliefs, and feelings to come through clearly to your mind. Acceptance of the world means letting your mind see the diversity of ideas and behaviors of other people. Many people refuse to accept themselves as they are because they do not want to face the challenge of changing themselves. An example will illustrate this point. A twenty-two-year-old man wanted to pursue a college degree. After taking a reading test, he discovered that he had an eighth-grade reading level. However, he did not believe the results of the test. He saw himself as a good reader capable of doing college work. Until that man accepted his reading deficiency, he could not advance his reading skill. Even with noble intentions about improving himself educationally, he was doomed to fail. You probably can think of several instances in your own life when you refused to accept some of your feelings and behavioral deficiencies. You chose instead to laugh them off or forget about them. You pretended that they were not part of you. But self-deception spawns confusion, and confusion cripples your emotional and mental life.

To avoid unnecessary pain, accept your feelings, ideas, and behavior, even the most embarrassing and uncomfortable ones. Likewise, remain open to the unwelcomed as well as the welcomed ideas and behavior of other people. If your ultimate goal is self-profit, that is, feeling good as a person, you need to know what is preventing you as well as what is helping you get what you want.

2. Analyze your behavior and feelings.

Take a close look at your negative feelings and behavior. Look at each type of behavior and feeling separately. Compare one instance with another. See if some hidden similarity emerges. For example, you may find out that each feeling of depression was preceded by someone saying something negative about you. Next, analyze your thinking at the time you were experiencing depression. What were you thinking when someone said something negative about you? You probably said, "He should not say that," "Maybe he's right," or "Who is she to say that?" In each of these statements you are really saying to yourself, "Everyone must say good things about me. I will not accept criticism." Feeling good about yourself, then, depends on people saying good things about you. Avoiding depression depends on how well you can control the remarks of other people.

As you analyze your feelings and behavior, you will find that your own thinking is most responsible for them. In this exercise you can root out all your negative ideas feeding your self-defeating feelings and behavior.

Most, if not all, your negative ideas, feelings, and behavior can be reduced to a view of life which says, "The world is not the way it should be." This complaint about life is really a protest against your responsibility to know yourself and the world as they are. This complaint is also an escape from exercising your freedom to change yourself and the world. As long as you point your finger at someone, you can avoid looking at yourself.

When you honestly accept yourself, and when you regularly analyze your thinking, you clear out those daily droning complaints. You feel free, light, and ready to do what is important.

3. Control your thoughts and behavior.

After you have discovered the negative ideas controlling your behavior and feelings, replace them with positive ideas. The particular ideas which you choose to direct your behavior will be shaped by your vision. When you ask yourself the following basic questions, you are developing a vision of life.

What is most important to me?

What is the meaning of my life?

Why do I try to live better each day?

Your vision of life will be your answers to these fundamental questions. You will know why you are living. Your goals will be clear.

For example, the meaning of your life might be to love your family and to grow in your profession. The particular ideas guiding your behavior toward your family might be respect, generosity, and openness. The ideas shaping your professional behavior might be diligence, prudence, and efficiency. Each day you practice these ideas at home and at work. Sometimes you do not know *how* to use these ideas. When you are aware that your ideas are not working out in your behavior, then you need more knowledge. You need to learn *how* to use your ideas to direct your behavior. Learning from a knowledgeable teacher how to use your mind to direct your behavior and feelings is education therapy.

4. Systematize your behavior.

Many of your daily actions will be done easily and calmly if each day you reflect on the meaning of your life and analyze your behavior and feelings. Your day will be systematized. To organize yourself does not mean to be routine or dull. It means that you arrange and guide all your actions according to what is important to you. If your day is not systematized, each little situation can become a crisis for you.

Because you know what is important to you, and you know how to use the correct ideas to get what you want, you are convinced that you are in charge of yourself. No matter what pops up in the course of a day, you can handle it. The following diagram illustrates this point.

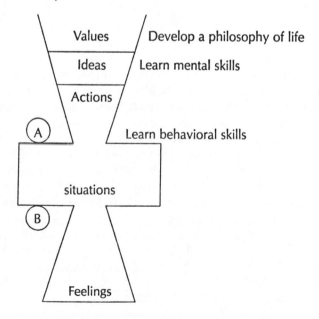

If the program written into the computer is broad enough, it will print out the correct answers to your questions. Likewise, if you develop a comprehensive philosophy of life, you can get meaningful answers for everyday situations. Your meaningful answer is your action at point A. Your feelings at point B will depend on your values and your ideas.

5. Decide practically.

To decide practically means to compare the consequences you want with consequences you might get from different actions. Many people assume that they need only the good intention to get what they want. Consequently, they pay little attention to choose the most appropriate behavior. They may know what is important to them, but they do not know how to change their ideal values into meaningful actions.

Practical decision-making is the bridge which allows your ideas to pass over into productive actions. Before acting, foresee the probable consequences of different forms of behavior in a situation. Choose the type of behavior which you believe will give you most of the consequences that you want. Remember that you cannot foresee all the consequences. Nevertheless, you will be satisfied with your decision if you clarified your values, analyzed yourself, and concentrated your attention on your choice.

Let us look at an example to illustrate practical decision-making. Bill was drafted into the army during the Vietnam war. Over the next two years he questioned the meaning of his life and the significance of the war. He was crystallizing a philosophy of life which was contradictory to his behavior as a soldier. He knew what consequences he wanted from his behavior. Convinced that he wanted to change his behavior, he reviewed a number of actions and their consequences which were open to him. The gamut ran from desertion to surrender as a conscientious objector. He chose to declare ·himself a conscientious objector and to accept the penalty of a two-year prison term.

Most of our decisions do not give us such uncomfortable effects. Bill's case is a good example to illustrate the strength of thinking in guiding behavior. Ultimately he experienced self-profit in his decision. He felt good about himself because his values, ideas, behaviors, and feelings were all together.

Other people in a situation similar to Bill's chose different actions. I know several young men who decided in good conscience to complete their tour of duty. They too went through a difficult and honest decision-making process. Their self-profit was also experiencing a unity of values, ideas, behavior and feelings.

15. The Point of Living

It was a rainy day. I was on my way to the college's administration building. At the end of the corridor I spotted Jim coming in my direction. Our paths had not crossed in a couple of weeks. After the usual college chatter Jim began to talk about his liking for farming. I asked him how he had become interested in agriculture. He told me that he had always wanted to be a farmer. However, twenty years ago when he had served in the navy as an enlisted man, he was struck by the difference in status between the officers and the enlisted men. He knew that education explained the difference, and he made up his mnd that he would get an education. He did. He achieved two master's degrees, one in mathematics and one in computer science. Now he was working in the college's computer center and doing some part-time teaching. From all outward appearances he was a successful man.

We continued our conversation about growth.

Jim said half-jokingly and half-seriously, "At the age of thirty-five I'm asking myself what I want to be when I grow up."

"It seems to me, Jim, that you're well settled." I sounded as if I were groping for some enthusiasm.

Jim became more serious "I have what I need. But in all these years I have never felt that I was growing."

"How is that?"

"What I really wanted to do, I didn't do. I did what I thought I was *supposed* to do—education and all that. After doing everything to get ahead, I thought that I would feel differently. I thought I would feel grown up, alive, fulfilled, and all that. But I don't feel as if I am growing. I simply feel that I'm doing a job, but all the time I'm looking for something else."

Within the past week you might have been involved in a similar conversation where you probably said or heard statements like:

"I feel stagnant."

"When I look around, everyone is moving ahead but I'm standing still."

"Time is slipping by and I haven't done a damn thing."

"I wish I had a job where I could grow."

If you reflect for a moment on these statements, you realize that "growth" is not an automatic process. If the growth that you are talking about takes place just by growing older, no one would be complaining. Consequently, you begin to wonder what growth really means.

Some erroneous assumptions about growth

Erroneous assumption #1: Viewing your life as a series of rigid stages.

You might believe that you should acquire certain possessions or character qualities by a certain age. If you are in your mid- or late-twenties without any foothold in a career, you are probably getting fidgety. You believe that by thirty you should have found your place in life.

If you are in your forties you might believe that your career, your family, and your personality should finally be established. When none of these is as firmly secure as you thought they would be, you begin to doubt that you have grown. Your feeling of not growing results from the erroneous assumption that your life is made up of a series of stages.

There is no external blueprint for your life. There are no real concrete stages out there. Stages do not make you. You make the stages. You determine the direction and rate of your growth.

Unless you are in control of your thinking, it is difficult to stop imagining your life as a staircase to happiness. It is common to think of yourself as being on a step or a rung of life. You probably think of others in a similar way. For example, the father excuses his son's behavior because "the boy is in that stage of life." In your own case you might excuse your own irresponsibility because you tell yourself, "I'm in that stage of life where you have to experience everything." Or you might be down on yourself because you feel, "In this stage of my life I should have accomplished something substantial. But what do I have to show?"

As long as you look at yourself *passing* through stages of life or going up the ladder or staircase of life, you will not feel that you are growing. You will simply feel that you are passing through, waiting to pass through, or putting up with passing through difficulties. Your life becomes one big sigh of relief heard in statements like:

"Thank God I got through school."

"I survived that relationship without too much damage."

"I finally got through the hassle of getting promoted."

"Somehow I pulled through all the changes of bringing up three kids."

Your common sense tells you that growing is a process of taking and giving. To live is to take what nature and people give you. Take a moment to reflect on what nature and people are presenting to your mind and body. Then think of what you are giving to nature and people. In this back and forth process you are creating ways to increase all the positive experiences of this interchange. For example, you want to increase peace, understanding, joy, and courage in your interpersonal relations. You will feel that you are growing if you view your life as an interchange of feelings, ideas, and behaviors with other people. You will behave productively and feel positively. Through your interchange with others you will expand your mind with new ideas, and you will strengthen your will and judgment by practicing your new ideas.

Erroneous assumption #2: Life is a problem to be solved.

You have heard the expression: "Life is one damn thing after another." When you translate that statement, "thing" means "problem." Some people believe that life is one big laboratory or classroom. Their life consists in getting 100% in problem-solving. For them, there is no mystery to life. There are only questions with right answers. If they are not coming up with the right answers they feel that they are not living. And it is easy to know when you have the right answer. Everything is in order. Everything fits. Everything balances. All the contradictions are eliminated. All the blanks are filled.

But in real life no one gets 100% in problem-solving. Life is not a problem to be solved. Neither is life a mystery to be lived. It is more accurate to say that life is a mystery to be solved. Problems have correct answers. You are either right or wrong. Mysteries have good and better answers. For example, there is no formula that tells you how to think and behave correctly toward your spouse. Love is a mysterious event. At times you believe you know much about it. At other times you believe you know little about love.

You have answers concerning your questions about the meaning of your life. Your answers can be better. As you improve your answers, you will feel that you are growing. You will know that you are growing because you will be doing, thinking, and feeling what is important to you.

Erroneous assumption #3: Life is a game to be played.

Is life basically competition? If your answer is yes, then you seriously look at life as a game. There are only winners and losers. The meaning of life is to know the ins and outs of the game and to play it better than anyone else. Winning demands practice to the point that you do not have to think about your own skills. Your mental activity is concentrated on your opponent. You must discover his or her weakness and then capitalize on it.

In the game of life the goal is success, which usually means money, prestige, and power. All the rules are found in the law books. The basic skills are shrewdness and aggressiveness.

Growth in the game of life is a matter of comparison. People believe they are growing because they have accumulated more money, prestige, and power than the average person. At other times they feel they are not growing because other people are getting ahead of them. These successful people have not lost any money or prestige; nevertheless, they feel they are going backward. This feeling is like sitting in a car waiting for the traffic light to change. While you remain stationary the car on your left moves ahead ten feet. You get the feeling you are going backward. Similarly, in the game of life you feel compelled to move first to stay ahead of your competitors.

If you believe that competition is the essence of life, you will probably feel that you are not growing most of the time. After a while you will play the game only where you can win. If you are not succeeding in the market, you will move the game into your home. Instead of loving your spouse and children you will compete with them.

Competition has a place in life but not the fundamental place. You can win without growing as a person. But if you grow as a person, success and winning will have a much broader meaning than money and prestige. For example, you can win the friendship of someone, but you can't buy it.

I want to grow means . . .

The widespread concern about personal growth is a recent phenomenon in American society. Words like human potential, self-actualization, a positive self, and fulfillment are heard in prisons, on the street corner, in board rooms, in factories, and on talk shows as well as in universities. If twenty-five years ago an employee complained to his supervisor that he was not being self-actualized in his job, his employer would have probably given him one of those "What the hell are you talking about?" looks. Today the supervisor understands the words because he has either learned elementary psychology at school or at the in-house education programs sponsored by his company. The employee in the 1970's is no longer met with a blank stare when he expresses his concern about his personal development; however, he still feels unfulfilled. Perhaps the pain of not feeling actualized is greater today than it was twenty-five years ago. You did not feel dejected if you did not know what you were missing. But today you cannot avoid knowing about self-actualization, self-fulfillment, being yourself, or growing to your full potential. Newspapers, books, magazines, and television will not let you escape their demands to become more than you are. Take a sampling of what you hear, see, and read in the next week. Observe the number of subtle ways that you are told to be more than you are. You can find the message particularly in commercials.

After being saturated with the philosophy of self-fulfillment you become convinced that you must grow. When you think about your growth as a person perhaps you feel simultaneously enthusiastic and frustrated. You know that you will enjoy yourself more if you improve yourself. But you might not know *what* personal growth means or *how* to achieve it. Because you feel a push from within you and a pull from everything around you saying "Grow up," you are ready to do almost anything that might help you grow. Some people go back to school, meet new people, take up hobbies, or change jobs. If you look closely at yourself, you can save yourself the pain of fruitless experimentation.

There is no better place to begin to understand personal growth than with yourself. The process of personal growth began within you when you felt the desire to grow. Let the process of growth continue within you by trying to answer your own questions. Some of your questions may be similar to the following:

1. "When I say I want to grow *what* do I mean?"
2. "*How* do I grow to become a full person?"
3. "*How do I know* that I am growing as a person?"

The following could be a series of internal dialogues between you as a seeker and as a finder trying to answer the three questions about growth.

What does personal growth mean?

Seeker: What is this growth and self-fulfillment everyone is talking about?

Finder: I don't know exactly, but I feel that there is something more to life than my day-to-day routine. Just doing what I am supposed to do gets boring.

Seeker: You mean that you feel you are withering away?

Finder: No, I'm not withering away. When I get up, I punch in to life, and when I go to bed at night, I punch out. One day seems like the next. There's nothing new from day to day.

Seeker: What can possibly be new? You live in the same house, with the same family, and you do the same work every day. Isn't it silly to be looking for something new? You wanted to be settled. Now that you're settled, you want to change.

Finder: In a way you are right. It doesn't make sense to change my job and all my relationships just because I'm bored. But I still feel the desire to experience novelty. Either the desire for newness is false and I have to forget about it, or the desire is true and I have to find a way to satisfy it.

Seeker: Maybe the question to ask yourself is *"Who* can be new?" instead of "What can be new?"

Finder: I get the point. If I want to experience novelty, *I* have to do something. *I* can be new each day. I can do things which I haven't done. I can think about new ideas. I can develop new attitudes. I can set up new goals for myself. I can discover new values. If I were to do all these things, I would feel that I am growing. My personal growth would mean that my values, my ideas, my feelings, and my behavior are being enriched and directed by my own mind.

Seeker: Do you believe that having more knowledge would make you feel fulfilled?

Finder: No, just knowing is not enough. I want to do something with the knowledge I've acquired. It seems to me that growing also means producing something. Usually all things which grow yield an offspring. I want my mental activities to create something. When I am using my mind and my body to make something, then I feel that I am growing. I feel that I am contributing something worthwhile to someone. I guess the best way to feel fulfilled is to create something and then share it. What I have made will become an occasion for someone else to grow. Artists and musicians must enjoy great satisfaction in knowing that their creations contribute to the growth of so many people.

Seeker: But you cannot create the way the artists and musicians do.

Finder: That's true. But I can know and appreciate beauty. I have to find a way to express it that fits my ability. I can also know truth and justice. I have to find a way to express them too. I feel myself becoming stronger when I am honest with myself and others. I can only grow, then, by being courageous, that is, by doing what I know is just and true. It is not difficult to know what is just and true. But it is difficult to do what I know. The whole matter of growing then means to be courageous.

Seeker: But where is this zig-zag conversation getting you? I thought you wanted to know what it means to grow.

Finder: Now I have a better understanding of growth and fulfillment. My personal growth means to deepen my understanding of what is important to me and to behave courageously. The entire process is simple and clear. I choose my values. I choose my actions. In so doing I freely make myself free. Nothing holds me back from growing as a person except my laziness and my fear.

How do you grow as a person?

Seeker: Your theory sounds sensible but it's one of those things which is easier said than done. Where do you start?

Finder: When I began to wonder about the meaning of my life, I asked myself what makes me different from everything else in the world. My answer was that no one sees me as I see myself, and no one sees the world as I see it. Although I can talk to other people about the same things, yet my mind can never become the property of anyone else. I came to the conclusion that my mind is one of a kind which cannot be taken away from me or even be given away by me. Every moment of my existence is truly my moment. It is up to me what I want to do with my time. I came to the realization that my feelings, my achievements, my failures, my goals, my values, and my growth all depended on knowing my own mind.

First, I had to know what my mind was capable of doing. When I blocked out all, or almost all, distractions, and concentrated on my ideas about life and death, I felt connected to everything alive. The feeling is similar to the one you experience at the theater or the symphony. You feel that you are part of the play or the music, but yet you know that you are separate from them. In this moment I knew and felt what was important to me—the reverence and cultivation of human life. All other values spin off this central theme.

I began to realize that man's mind is more than intelligence. The mind of the simple peasant could see and understand more about life than the noted professor. The most intelligent are not necessarily the wisest. Any person who chooses to meditate on life and death will discover the powers of his or her own mind.

Seeker: You are not answering my question. You already said that growth means deepening one's understanding and behaving courageously, but *how* do you do these things?

Finder: Once I knew that my mind could do more than juggle ideas, I began to practice what it can do, that is, meditate. First, I would get rid of all distractions. Second, I would focus my attention on one of my ultimate concerns, such as life and death, eternity, justice, and love.

By doing this daily, I clearly saw what is important to me. Now to get to your question. If I want to grow, I ought to meditate daily. If I want to behave courageously I ought to keep my mind on what is important to me before I act.

Seeker: Don't you think that your theory is too general? For example, how do you deal with a boss who is authoritarian and abusive?

Finder: You chose a good example, because I had a boss like that. He was always cutting people down. If I focused my attention on his behavior toward me, I would get upset. Then I didn't know what to do because I was rattled. But when I focused my attention on what was important to me, I was able to control the situation.

Living justly or respecting every person including myself is important to me. My intention was to get him to behave respectfully toward me. I was working in the office for six months when he tried his intimidation act on me. He barked at me to come into his office. Then he began shouting about my absence from the office on the preceding day. I quietly closed the door to his office, looked him straight in the eye without blinking, and told him in an even and determined tone that I could not understand what he was saying because he was talking too loud. Then I asked him if he would kindly repeat what he had on his mind. He did, and in a reasonable tone. That was the first and last time he tried to intimidate me. From then on we got along well.

As long as I kept my mind on what was important to me, my actions came easily and naturally.

Seeker: Are you trying to tell me that all you have to do is know what is important to you in order to grow and enjoy life?

Finder: Knowing what is important to me is the first step toward personal growth. But each day I have to practice what is important to me. I improve my judgment by choosing to do what is valuable to me. Provided I clearly know what I want, I will behave wisely and productively.

Seeker: But many people do not get what they believe is important to them.

Finder: Then they have fooled themselves. It's easy to *say* that a career, a relationship, money, freedom, and trust are important. But true importance means that I work hard at achieving what is important to me. And working hard means that I direct my mind and body to learn the ways to accomplish what I want.

Seeker: Then the answer to my question about *how* to grow as a person is to *know* what is important to you and to *choose* to do what is important to you.

Finder: There are other things to do, but knowing and choosing form the heart of personal growth. By knowing I mean insight or intuition. What I see seizes and energizes me. For example, if I truly know someone well from the inside, I feel his or her presence inside myself. My whole being is stimulated by his or her presence. Knowing what is important to me has the same effect. Choosing to behave according to what is important to me comes easily because I clearly see what I want.

Seeker: For example, if I want to be a lawyer, a college graduate, or even a rich person, I can easily learn what I have to learn to become any one of them.

Finder: That's right. The learning will come easier than you realize. The difficult part is the energy, sweat, and time that you have to invest in order to get what you want.

How do you really know if you are growing?

Seeker: You said before that people can easily fool themselves. They pretend that they are fulfilling themselves by always talking about the importance of personal growth. Did you ever feel that way?

Finder: That's true. I talked myself sick about growing as a person. I put on a good appearance, but my deepest feelings told me that I was lying to myself.

Seeker: How can you tell if you are growing or deceiving yourself?

Finder: I fooled myself into thinking that I was growing because I was making plenty of money. I have everything that comes with money. My possessions are still growing, but I don't feel any movement within myself. I know what it means to be rich, but I don't know what it means to be human. With all my possessions I am a very insecure individual. The meaning of my life depends on what I own.

Seeker: Surely you must feel good about all your successes.

Finder: That's true. I worked hard to get what I have. But I was also lucky when I started my business. Nevertheless, making money is one thing, and making myself a full person is another.

Seeker: Are you saying that you do not feel good about yourself?

Finder: That's half right. I feel good about myself as a businessman. I am competent, efficient, and aggressive. I can handle any situation; however, inside I am restless and discontented. I want my mind and emotional life to mature. I feel that my life means more than what I am doing. But I don't know what I am reaching for.

Seeker: What is important to you?

Finder: Obviously, money is, and all the things you have to do to get it. However, freedom is very important to me also.

Seeker: What does freedom mean to you?

Finder: To choose to be the person I want to be.

Seeker: And who do you want to be?

Finder: I want to be a joyful, creative, wise, and magnanimous person.

Seeker: You mean being rich is not enough for you?

Finder: It's enough for anyone who only wants money. But I want to feel some movement inside myself. I want to feel that I am in control of my life. Too often my actions and my feelings are determined by what is happening around me. I look as though I am in charge of my life, but in reality I am usually just reacting to people and events around me. I spend most of my energy to control other people. But I don't have a grip on my own life. At this point, I am asking myself what I am living for.

Seeker: Have you found a satisfying answer to your question?

Finder: When I think about myself I realize that I have the power to do almost anything. My power is my ability to choose. I can choose to jump off a bridge, to study for a profession, to open a business, to love someone, to harm someone, to make money, to write a book, to read a book, to have children, etc. The power to choose the life I want is tremendous. But if I don't know what is important to me as a person this power is destructive. In my decisions I am making or breaking myself as a person. When I act without thinking about my personal values, I usually do something stupid. I feel out of tune with myself. On the other hand, when I do what is valuable to me, I feel like a full and vibrant person.

Seeker: Are you saying that your reason for living each day is to know and to do what is important to you?

Finder: That's right. As long as I am expanding my vision of what is valuable to me as a person, and as long as I am acting on what is important to me, I feel that I am growing.

Seeker: What does growing feel like?

Finder: It's like the feeling you get when you find your way after having been lost. Several times I was lost in the traffic of big cities and a few times in the mountains. I felt forlorn and confused. Then I would recognize a landmark which set me on my way. My mind was relieved. I moved freely and easily toward my destination.

The feeling of growing is the feeling of confidence which comes from knowing what you want, and it is the feeling of strength which comes from deciding to push yourself to get what you want. The feeling of growing is also the feeling of novelty which comes from learning new ideas and behaviors.

Seeker: Which feeling comes first?

Finder: The feeling of confidence. When I took time out to look inside myself, I found that my power to be who I wanted to be rested in my own mind and will. All the knowledge I had about human behavior meant nothing unless I knew what to use it for.

Seeker: Did you behave any differently when you felt as though you were growing?

Finder: Day after day I found myself behaving with greater ease. I was less anxious and irritable. I was beginning to enjoy every day.

Maybe I can express this feeling of exhilaration by using tennis as an example. When I was learning to play tennis I felt awkward. I thought I would never learn because too many things required my concentration—how to hold the racquet, how to switch grips, how to negotiate the backhand swing. When I concentrated on one thing I forgot the other. I knew how to do each movement separately, but I could not put them all together. Instead of concentrating on each motion I decided to envision myself as the tennis player I wanted to be. Then I kept my eyes riveted on the ball. Within a few months everything fell in place. I began to enjoy the game immensely. If I had continued to pay attention to each individual motion, I would still be awkward on the court.

Learning to behave effectively begins inside myself. When I see what I want, then I can clearly see how to act. I know that I am growing because my mind, my will, my behaviors and my feelings are all going after what is important to me.

Putting it all together

"What a beautiful family!"
"What a beautiful machine!"
"What a beautiful person!"

"That is beautiful!"

"What a beautiful concert!"

"What beautiful work!"

Day in and day out you hear exclamations about beauty. You immediately know what someone means by "What a beautiful person!" You find it easy to recognize beauty in people and things around you. But have you ever been aware of beauty in yourself? How many times have you said:

"What a beautiful person I am!"

"What beautiful work I do!"

"What beautiful feelings I create in myself!"

"What a beautiful decision I made!"

When you think that you are not beautiful, that your feelings, thoughts, decisions, and behaviors are plain, then ask yourself what beauty means to you. Reflect for a moment on a beautiful sunset, a beautiful concert, and a beautiful person.

The sunset speaks to you. "I am majestic. I am warm. I embrace the earth. I am powerful. I am genuine. I am changing, but I am the same. I am here each day, but I'm never boring."

The concert speaks to you. "I am harmony. I am vibrant. I am soft. I am strong. I am sad. I am wild. I am new each time you hear me. I am the same concert but I am different."

The beautiful person speaks to you in his actions. "I am the sunset. I am the concert."

When you say that a person is beautiful you mean that you see in his words, his actions, his feelings, and his thoughts the person that you want to be. And that person is one who is strong and tender, wise and respectful, humorous and serious, changing and the same. The beautiful person is the one who harmonizes all his activities around the theme of love. He cares about the growth of his own life and all life around him. Caring means that he acts positively. When you spot such a human being you say, "That person has got *it* all together."

What is the it?

When you say that a person has it all together, that "it" means his ideas, feelings, emotions, behaviors, and values. The all-together person is like a walking sunset, a traveling concert or a finely tuned machine. He weaves his ideas, emotions, and behaviors into patterns which elegantly express his values.

The all-together person is the growing person. The personal growth process begins when you accept your responsibility to know yourself. The first step in knowing yourself is to accept your positive and negative tendencies. The second step in knowing yourself is to use your mind to guide your behaviors according to your positive tendencies. When you work with something, you learn more about it. For example, the motor of a car may be a big mystery to you until you get under the hood to take it apart and put it back together. Your mind, which is the motor of your life, is always a mystery. However, you can know your own mind more and more only by working with it to discover the meaning of life. The following outline illustrates what you see or hear when you take a look into your own mind.

Irrational tendencies—"I'm feeling bad."

> Confusion—"I feel mixed up."
> Dependence—"I feel pinned down."
> Rebellion—"I don't give a damn about anyone or anything."
> Doubt—"I feel that I can't trust anyone."
> Self-destruction—"I feel that living is not worth the effort."

Rational tendencies—"I'm feeling okay."

> Order—"I feel that I'm getting my life together."
> Control—"I feel that I am in charge of myself."
> System—"I feel that my life is running nicely."
> Certainty—"I feel confident about what I am doing."
> Self-profit—"I feel that I'm getting what I want."

Supra-rational tendencies—"I feel great."

> Vision—"I see what is important and valuable to me."
> Freedom—"I feel light, powerful, and determined to do what is important."
> Change—"I feel deeper, richer, and broader as a person after every important change in my life."

Conclusion - In a Nutshell

In this book I have stated that your feelings, behaviors, and ideas are explained by your irrational, rational and more than rational tendencies. You can know all of these tendencies. They exist *simultaneously*. You can also know what tendency is at work in you at any given time. Even more important you can *choose* which tendency will be the center of your life.

Your irrational tendencies

Let's begin with your irrational tendency to be confused. You express your confusion in such statements as: "I just don't know what to do." "I don't know what's wrong." "The more I try, the worse it gets." You are unable to support a state of confusion too long, because you cannot stand the mental anguish and physical suffering that come in its wake. You are willing to become dependent on a pain-killer to escape the agony. Sometimes you lean on another person to escape your own insecurity. At another time the dependency may be drink, drugs, sex, or sleep. When none of these crutches cures the malady of confusion, you rebel against yourself and everyone around you. When you are worn out from your rebellion you slip into the shadows of skepticism. As soon as the

183

glimmering rays of hope fade, you plunge yourself into despair and ultimately into self-destruction.

Irrational tendencies are steps to self-destruction.

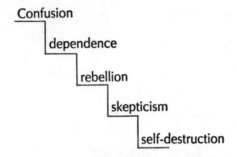

It's all downhill.

Your rational tendencies

Fortunately, you also have rational tendencies. Instead of escaping confusion through dependency, you try to reason your way toward establishing an acceptable order in your behavior. Confusion is the cue that tells you something is wrong. You decide to correct the wrong by searching for a principle that will guide your future behavior. The principle may be a rule of conduct drawn from religion or philosophy. For example, your marriage vows may keep your life free from falling into side affairs. You minimize your conflicts by being consistently obedient to your religious or philosophical discipline. As long as you follow your rules of behavior, you experience a feeling of self-control. After experiencing this positive feedback from obeying a rule, you then attempt to systematize all your future behavior according to a pattern of basic principles. Because you believe that you can predict the consequences of your actions you feel certain about yourself. Preferring to be happy rather than miserable, you, the ordered person, will choose those actions that will be of profit to you.

Your supra-rational tendencies

In general, when you follow your rational tendencies you will feel satisfaction, provided the basic principles which establish order in your life are also compatible with your supra-rational tendencies. Let's illustrate this point with the example of marriage. Often the marriage vows, which you view as principles of order leading you to happiness, can be a harness preventing you from acting freely and responsibly. You may have become unduly dependent on your spouse and the habits of marriage, yet you use your rational tendencies to justify this irrational dependency. Marriage vows, as principles of order, make sense if the partners grow in vision, freedom, and creativity. You can see, then, that your rational tendencies are insufficient in themselves to account for your happiness. The realities related to your supra-rational tendencies, though less immediately apparent to you, are the true goals of your rational processes. Your three options are: (1) to use your rational tendencies to support your irrational tendencies; (2) to use your rational tendencies so that the perfection of order and control themselves become the goals of your life; (3) to use your rational tendencies to develop your supra-rational tendencies.

Have you ever had a clear vision of the meaning of your life? If not a clear vision, have you ever had at least a recognition that the meaning of life is more than the daily routine of eating, sleeping, and going to work? Even a vacation, in itself, does not make sense if it is only an escape from a senseless routine. When you entertain questions about the meaning and importance of life, you begin to experience your supra-rational tendency of vision. Your responses to these questions are your reasons for getting up in the morning and enjoying life. There are no ready-made answers. Each individual develops a statement about life which satisfies his or her own degree of curiosity. What is important to people depends on a variety of circumstances—childhood experiences, financial situation, present emotional state, relationships with other people, and the perception of oneself. But no matter what the situation, everyone at some time will ask: What is important to me?

Freedom follows the content of vision. You will no longer feel constrained in your actions. As soon as you know what is important, you will take charge of your own behavior. The desire to secure what is valuable to you, rather than your obsession for approval or your fear of rejection, will guide your actions.

You begin to see that life is similar to the movement of breathing. You absorb what is around you. You change what you have assimilated. You give something back to the environment. Each moment of life is change and each change can be an experience of spontaneity and novelty. For example, interpersonal relationships are not set once and for all. Each individual has a tendency to see more and become more in himself or herself. This tendency causes a relationship to constantly change. Consequently, each other's behavior is not completely predictable. Accepting change as the essence of life adds an exciting quality to a relationship, whereas inability to accept change introduces anxiety to the relationship.

Once you have responded to the tendencies of vision, freedom, and change, you will be creative. How often have you been bored with your relationships, with your job, or with yourself? You were bored each time you looked for something or someone exciting to break the monotony. However, the new face or the novel event was only a fleeting moment of pleasantness making your relapse into ennui more painful. Your search for novelty everywhere except in yourself is your routine error. When you choose to do what is important to you, you begin to feel alive. That course you wanted to take, you take. That business you wanted to start, you start. That poem you wanted to write, you write. That behavior you wanted to change, you change. Each decision you make and each type of behavior you perform are steps in the creation of your life.

Finally, to grow as a human being is no automatic process. Your emotional, intellectual, and social development depends on your vision of yourself and your courage to make that vision come true in your actions.

How to live a better life

You know that you exist from day to day to live better, yet you do not exactly know what "better" means. Some days "better" means to make more money. Other days "better" means to experience some inner peace. And yet other days "better" means to get along pleasantly with people. If you have settled on what "better" means, then you are faced with the question "how." How do I make more money? How do I achieve inner peace? How do I get along with people? If you have a comprehensive view of yourself, you will be able to answer these questions and you will achieve your goals. Once you know all the tendencies of your mind, you are free to do what you want. You can determine specifically for yourself what a better life means and how to achieve it. But the first step in living a better life is knowing your mind.

Each tendency is accompanied by specific behaviors, feelings, and ways of thinking. Your knowledge of yourself and others depends on what tendencies influence your attention. The following diagram illustrates this point. Suppose you are at point A and you view the world, events and people at point C, through the square of skepticism on the grid.

Irrational	Rational	Supra-Rational
confusion	order	vision
dependence	control	freedom
rebellion	system	change
skepticism	certainty	creativity
self-destruction	self-profit	growth

Probably you are skeptical because you were overly dependent on someone, some ideal, or some organization which failed you in your moment of need. Then you rebelled against them for not being trustworthy. Finally, you generalized your mistrust of some people to all people. If you had chosen to view the world through the window of freedom, you would have allowed yourself and others some room for change without becoming mistrustful. You would have been on the road to growth instead of self-destruction. Unless you are aware of all your tendencies, you develop a biased view of yourself and others. It is worth taking a chance to see yourself and others differently.

Your tendencies fall into three groups: irrational, rational, and supra-rational. They exist simultaneously within you. When you experience an irrational tendency you can offset it by being attentive to its adjacent rational and supra-rational tendency. When you experience a rational tendency, find out if your rational processes are supporting your irrational or supra-rational tendencies. Your supra-rational tendencies will account for your happiness.

The challenge to behave as the insightful, responsible, tolerant, free and creative person that you are potentially confronts you each day. If you listen carefully to yourself, you will find the meaning of your life in the dialogue between you and you.